I, MON

positive ways of working with challenging teens through understanding the adolescent within us

David Taransaud

Speechmark

I, MONSTER

positive ways of working with challenging teens
through understanding the adolescent within us

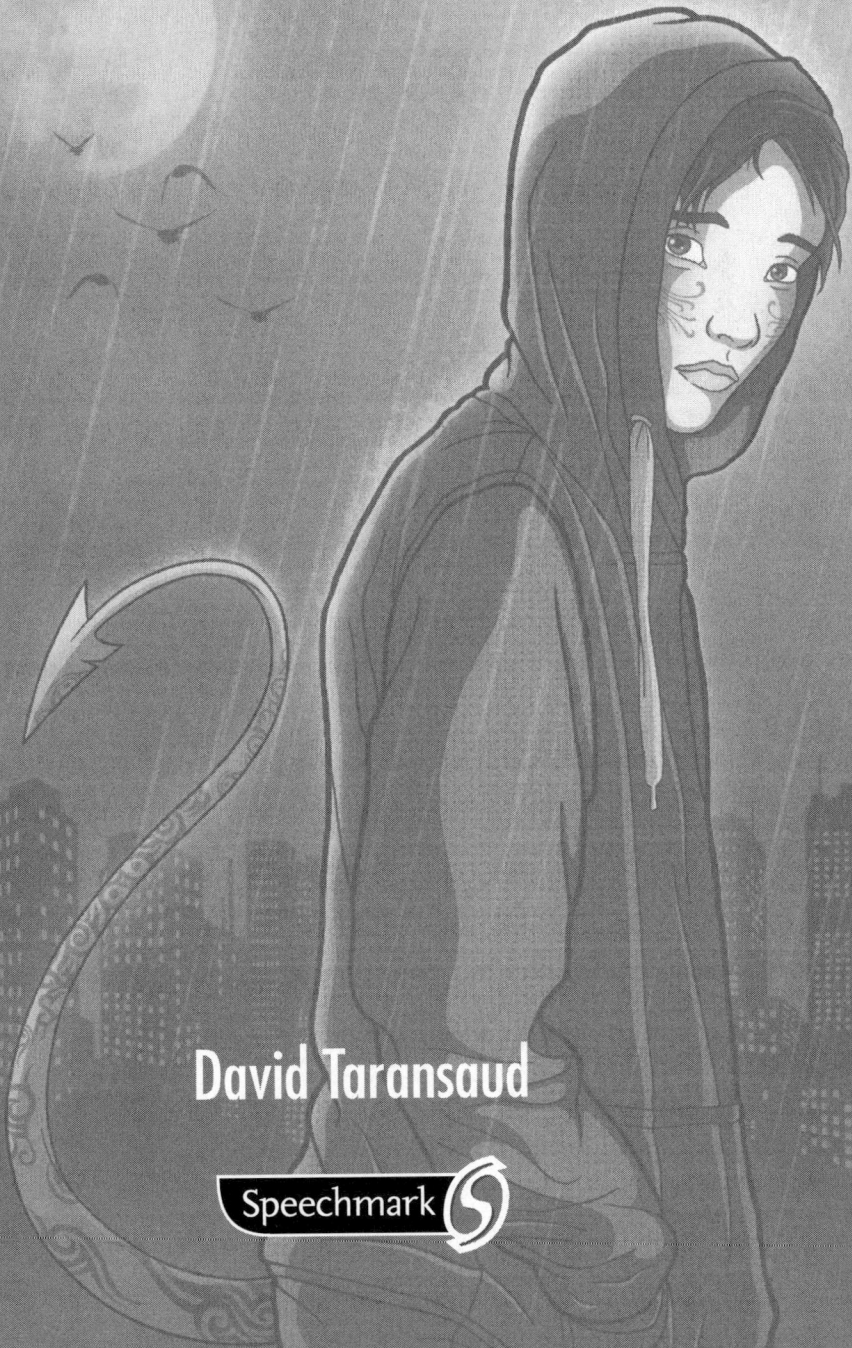

David Taransaud

Speechmark

For my mother

First published in 2016 by
Speechmark Publishing Ltd,
2nd Floor, 5 Thomas More Square, London E1W 1YW, UK
Tel: +44 (0)845 034 4610; Fax: +44 (0)845 034 4649
www.speechmark.net

Design and artwork by Moo Creative (Luton)
Front cover by David Taransaud

002-6044/Printed in the United Kingdom by CMP (uk) Ltd

British Library Cataloguing in Publication Data
A catalogue record for this book is available from the British Library

ISBN 978 1 91118 606 9

Inside all of us is hope
Inside all of us is fear
Inside all of us is adventure
Inside all of us is a wild thing.

Where the Wild Things Are
Warner Bros, 2009
Directed by S. Jonze

CONTENTS

Note on the Text. For the sake of clarity alone, throughout this text 'he' is used to refer to the child or adolescent under discussion.

ACKNOWLEDGEMENTS

I have many debts of gratitude to acknowledge. My greatest thanks and love go to the young people who shared their realities with me in words, pictures and silences. I am especially grateful to the Kitgum's orphans in Uganda and the street kids at the Alleviate Addiction Suffering Trust in Karachi. Thank you for teaching me the true meaning of forgiveness, faith and dignity.

I am deeply indebted to my supervisor, Ursula Deniflee, and to all my tutors at the Institute for Arts in Therapy and Education, foremost Dr Margot Sunderland, for her generosity and unwavering passion, and Dr Dan Hughes, for his unfailing empathy and immense humanity.

I also wish to acknowledge one of the most caring and inspirational head teachers I have met: Toni Munoz Bailey from Chaigeley School. Thank you for restoring my faith in education and for creating a safe space where vulnerable young people can rediscover their potential for growth and happiness.

Many thanks must also go to Sarah Dessent for her incisive insight and her invaluable editing advice throughout the process of writing *I, Monster*; Erum Khan Ghazi for her inspired suggestions, her friendship and fierce determination; A. R. Allana for showing me that the deepest wounds can heal and mountains can be moved, one rock at a time; and Richard Akena whose courage and dedication to those who have been hurt is equal to none.

Finally, I would like to acknowledge the friends and colleagues who welcomed me into their hearts and encouraged me to let go of the familiar: Frances Ackland-Snow, Samia Chundrigar, Shamyla Khan, Layla Lodhia, Haya Salim and Yoko Ueda. Thank you for loving me at my worst and teaching me that being a little monster can be a lot of fun.

INTRODUCTION

Monsters, the Disavowed Children of the Human Mind

Monsters are our Others par excellence.
Without them we know not what we are.
With them we are not what we know.

Richard Kearney

(*Strangers, Gods and Monsters*, 2003, p117)

Originally developed to repel roaches, rodents and other unwanted pests, sonic weapons have recently been repurposed to target teenagers. The MK-4, also known as the 'Mosquito Teen Repellent', is a small box-like device that emits an ear-splitting 17-kilohertz noise only audible to people under the age of 25.[1] The UK device manufacturer claims it is *'the only product on the market that has the teeth to bite back at these kids'*.[2] By making the most of age-related hearing loss, the sonic deterrent creates zones of discomfort intense enough to dissuade troublesome teenagers from congregating in public places. But the anti-loitering MK-4 does not target behaviour; it targets youths indiscriminately. The manufacturer's sales brochure certifies it is *'100% legal to own and to use [...] No licenses or permissions required'*, and *'the UK Home Office even support[s] the use of the device'*.[3] Since it first went on sale in January 2006, thousands of devices have been purchased by homeowners, shopkeepers, as well as police forces and councils. Although an investigation by the Council for Europe found that the MK-4 violates

---

[1] For those of us who are above 25, an audible version of the Mosquito tone is available on http://www.freemosquitoringtones.org/

[2] http://www.compoundsecurity.co.uk/

[3] In February 2010, North East Derbyshire MP Natascha Engel told the House of Commons that if the device were to target any other marginal group, we would cry out discrimination. When she asked for the MK-4 to be banned, Home Secretary Alan Johnson replied: *'I'm personally committed to using any device that has been proved to [...] help to bring about the improvement in behaviour that we are all seeking'* (https://www.youtube.com/watch?v=4Ju8mJWXVBM).

legislation prohibiting torture, and thus should be banned, the UK has more Mosquitos in use than any other European state (Townsend, 2010).

However, shortly after the anti-teen repellent was introduced to the market, young people reclaimed the high-pitched sound and used it as a ringtone allowing them to secretly receive text messages during lessons. It seems that all the MK-4 managed to achieve is to further widen the divide between generations.

Many of us suffer from ephebiphobia – an irrational fear of youths, says psychologist Dr Tanya Byron (2009b).[4] We see children as pestilent and treat them like vermin. Yet research suggests that our anxieties are fuelled by the media's eagerness to demonise all young people as gun-toting hoodies rather than actual encounters with crime (Clark, 2011; Burton, 2012). The Women in Journalism report[5] (Bawdon, 2009) states that although there is some news coverage where adolescents are described in glowing terms, such as 'model student' or 'every mother's perfect son', these descriptions are reserved for those who have met a violent and untimely death. Young people are rarely seen in a positive light in the press and regularly find themselves at the receiving end of the 'monster' epithet. As Gitta Sereny aptly remarks, 'tabloids have not progressed from the medieval conviction of evil birth; they do not believe in traumatized children' (1998, p388). These adolescents are not soulless savages. They are survivors of adverse childhood experiences; their 'monstrous' behaviour is a reflex response to vulnerability and insecurity. It is the means by which they manage early terrors and conceal the shamed and hurt aspect of their self. They are children whose sense of self and trust have been violated by the people they once depended upon.

---

[4] Byron describes an ephebiphobic society as one 'that views young people in negative and judgmental terms, where the media report (with barely disguised glee) the latest hideous crimes and abuses of our young [...] But this fear and suspicion are counterproductive. If you tell someone they are a failure enough times, they will be' (The Telegraph, 17 March 2009a).

[5] The Women in Journalism (WiJ) report tracked newspaper stories about teens across the national and regional press. They found that the words most commonly used to describe young people were (in descending order of frequency) 'yobs, thugs, sick, feral, hoodie, louts, heartless, evil, frightening, scum, monsters, inhuman and threatening' (2009, p9).

They are children who learned that love only brings pain and intimacy goes hand in hand with abuse. They are emotional orphans who grew up expecting the worst from others, and sadly many of us exceed their expectations.

Consider the following: '*I'm a teacher and sometimes I'd like nothing more than to punch a kid right in the face … and laugh*'. This comment is one of the many entries made on Whisper, a social network that allows people to make anonymous confessions. Other Whisper users admit:

> *Whenever I'm wrong and a student corrects me I find a way to punish him or her without letting it be obvious.*

> *I hate to admit that I hate these kids sometimes … and by sometimes I mean usually.*

> *Whenever a student I hate turns in a paper I throw it out and blame it on them.*

> *As a teacher, I have to admit sometimes I wish I could deduct points from a kids average for being a jerk.*

Haven't we all entertained such hostile fantasies towards the most challenging young people in our care? I certainly have. We all have aggression to spare, notes Mansfield: '*We keep it in stock so as to have it ready when it is needed and even, or especially, when it is unneeded and unwanted; [we] offer it on slight occasions as a free gift, useful or not*' (2006, p64). And although most of us are too conscientious to act out our destructive impulses, our capacity for immoral sentiments and acts, and our awareness of that capacity, tell us that darkness is not just out there; it is an inherent part of who we are (Rothman, 2011).

In *Inside the Magic Rectangle*, newspaper columnist Victor Lewis-Smith (1995) mentions a placard at London zoo that invites passers-by to stick their heads through a hole, oblivious to the fact that a sign on the other side reads: 'Man, the most dangerous animal of all'. Maybe the sign should read: 'Man, the most destructive and self-deceiving creature that has ever walked the earth', for deep beneath our sophisticated and civilised exterior lies primitive impulses, unmet needs and repressed desires: the unwanted and unloved parts of ourselves that still yearn for restoration and validation. And the more we deny our secret self, the more likely we are to project onto others what we fear within or the more likely we are to condemn in them what we can't admit in ourselves, for what is love-starved seeks the illusion of power. It finds targets in others and often constitutes the basis of hatred, prejudice and violence (Bradshaw, 1988).

So to reflect upon the monstrous behaviour is to ponder that side of our selves which we conceal beneath our well-worn social masks (Nelson, 2010). As Weinstock asserts, 'the monster tells us what we hope or imagine we are not, as well as what we fear deep down we are or may become [...] Monsters are always inevitably the disowned and disavowed children of the human mind' (2014, p3). They are our night selves. They are our unloved and unlived parts that sometimes return in dark disguises. And therefore to truly face the monster, we must engage the otherness within and embrace the totality of ourselves. But uncovering all that hides under the floorboards in the dark cellar of the psyche and not knowing what is going to emerge can feel like a terrifying gamble. It is a risk we have to take, for if our love cannot extend to the broken and estranged parts of our selves, neither can it extend to those who have been labelled 'monster' (Hillman, 1999).

The chapters[6]

In their collection of essays on monsters, Davis and Santos ask: 'Is the monster apart from, or a part of the self?' (2010, ix). This book is written

---

[6] An earlier and combined version of chapters 8 and 9 was published in the BACP magazine Children and Young People under the title 'Savage Beasts'. June 2012.
An earlier and shorter version of chapter 11 was published in the BAPT magazine Play Therapy. Issue 75, Autumn 2013.
An earlier and shorter version of chapter 12 was published in the BACP magazine Children and Young People under the title 'Who Wants to be a Superhero?' March 2013.
An earlier and shorter version of chapter 20 was published in the BAPT magazine Play Therapy under the title 'Reality, a Thing of the Past'. Issue 80, Winter 2014.
All of these have been revised and updated for the purpose of this book.

from my strong belief that it is both, and that the only way to form an alliance with adolescents locked in an illusion of superiority is to first reacquaint ourselves with the wild things that lurk within all of us. The origin of the word 'monster' can be traced back to the Latin *monstrum*: 'a curious object of both dread and fascination that disrupts the social order'. *Monstrum* originates from *monstrare*: 'that which reveals and instructs', which in turn derives from *monere*: 'to warn'. The monster narratives discussed throughout this book warn, reveal and instruct. They warn against turning our back on our unloved and unlived self. They reveal what lies beneath the monstrous behaviour of the troubled teen, and they inform our approach to support him to develop more positive patterns of relating. They are, for the majority, tales of a dark and cautionary kind. They are not always stories in which everybody lives happily ever after, but they are important ones, for they carry the truth.

I, Monster is divided into three parts. Part 1 suggests that our greatest foes do not hide beneath baseball caps and hooded tops but lurk deep within ourselves and that knowing our own darkness is the best method for dealing with the darkness of other people (Jung, 1973). Part 2 focuses on the dynamics that take place within the inner world of adolescents who use aggression to manage early terrors. Part 3 explores strategies to help them heal the pain of the past and support them find their way back on the road of creative living.

Chapters 1 and 2 introduce the concept of the Shadow, our darker twin and the personification of '*everything that the subject refuses to acknowledge about himself and yet is always thrusting itself upon him directly or indirectly*' (Jung, 1963, p399). They explore the similarities between the changes in midlife and the individuation process during adolescence and conclude that working with wounded young people is likely to reawaken painful elements of our own history. In short, these chapters suggest that the work with adolescents also becomes a work on ourselves (Frankel, 1998) and that before we reach out to them, we need to reach in.

Chapters 3 and 4 examine how, in spite of our wish to remain professional, unprocessed emotional memories can impact upon the way in which we interact with vulnerable young people. They demonstrate how developing our ability to be open and sensitive to the unpredicted and unexpected within ourselves allows us to communicate to others that impulsive urges can be survived rather than acted out. In other words, they argue that the best place to deal with an aggressive teenager is not in the classroom or in the dust of the playground, but in our own mind (Bernstein, 2001).

Chapter 5 begins by asking a question: are fears innate or learned? It goes on to describe how most of our fears are signals by which we notice what we have not yet integrated (Richo, 1997). They belong to the affection-starved child in all of us who still longs for a loving and consistent caregiver. Finally, it explains that to be free from the burden of the past and reclaim all that is deep within us is not a solitary endeavour; it is a long and arduous journey that requires not only a process of remembering but also the presence of an empathic witness willing to make a journey similar to ours.

Chapter 6 argues that to work with emotionally wounded young people, we need to be more than healers, teachers, providers or counsellors; we ought to be 'fellow travellers' (Yalom, 2002). We must show them the way through personal modelling, and of course, we can only help them to go as far as we ourselves have gone or are willing to go.

We will conclude the first part of *I, Monster* by examining how cycles of abuse and relational failures echo across generations. Chapter 7 looks at the adults who are part of the troubled adolescent's immediate environment and explains why we need to join forces with them. Two case studies invite us to reframe our perceptions of 'bad' parents and suggest creative ways of working with them. For unless we provide empathic support to emotionally wounded mothers and fathers, they'll pass on their legacy of pain to their own children, and history will repeat itself.

The second part of this book takes us into the inner world of traumatised teens. It argues that turning into a monster is not always the end of self, and once we understand there is a suffering child behind the apparent monstrous behaviour, we open the possibility of reaching out to such a child (Horney, 1945).[7] Concentrating on Sendak's masterpiece, *Where the Wild Things Are* (1963), and McKee's picture book *Not Now Bernard* (1980), chapters 8 and 9 investigate the purpose of fantasy and imaginative play for the securely attached child and for the one raised in a cold and unresponsive environment. They conclude that in the absence of warmth, safety and appropriate maternal care, children surrenders their autonomy to a powerful bestial substitute and become the victim of their fiction.

Chapter 10 investigates the life of Dennis Avner – or, as he preferred to be called, 'Stalking Cat' – a survivor of child sexual abuse who surgically altered his body to resemble that of his totem animal, the tiger. His life story will further our understanding of the survival strategies a child employs when the people who are supposed to keep him safe are the cause of his distress.

Chapters 11–13 look at the task of identity formation during adolescence. They argue that although adolescent rebellion is a manifestation of a drive towards selfhood, for young people whose sense of worth and safety have been shattered, aggression is about survival and hope. Not only is it an out-of-date response to the intense fear they experienced in their formative years, it is also a distress call. It is how they seek the acceptance and security that their early environments failed to provide.

Chapters 14 and 15 focus on the critical role of touch and holding (both physical and symbolic) for healthy emotional development and neurobiological growth. They describe how an empathic embrace can

---

[7] Some of the themes discussed in this section have previously been explored in my book *You Think I'm Evil* (2011). I return to them here and explore them further through a different lens, that of stories about youth culture.

reawaken attachment needs and put psychological development back on track.

Chapter 16 argues that it is through compassion that suffering can find an outlet and be transformed. It illustrates the difficulties of maintaining an empathic and authentic presence while on the receiving end of challenging behaviour. It also provides practical strategies on how to connect with young people's vulnerability and how to be more in sync with ours.

Chapter 17 first investigates the lives of Joe Coleman (a Brooklyn artist) and Mary Bell (the 11-year-old girl who in 1968 killed two boys of four and three and was demonised across the country as a child monster). It then focuses on the healing power of the Arts. It describes how the process of art making, together with the facilitation of a safe and reliable environment, can help adolescents re-author their painful past experiences into a coherent narrative that is no longer about shame and humiliation.

The previous points are further illustrated in chapter 18 which also highlights that symbolic expression is a rich window to the world of wounded individuals, and with adolescents it is often the only window available to us (Riley & Malchiodi, 1999). Finally, it describes how the Arts help build a working alliance with adolescents who approach love with one foot on the accelerator and the other one on the brake.

Chapter 19 brings together all the approaches and theories discussed so far. It also provides strategies on how to survive potentially explosive encounters with adolescents who use rage to compensate for overwhelming feelings of fear and worthlessness.

Finally, the last two chapters focus on the conflicts that rage within the young person's inner world. They suggest that to restore peace in a war-torn inner landscape, the competing forces must be encouraged to interact with each other and 'speak their minds' until they can rediscover their original state of togetherness.

The point which I hope you will come across is that *I, Monster* is first and foremost a book about hope and transformation, for monsters are liminal creatures. They have the power to overthrow cognitive barriers, to reconcile opposites and to unite past and present, known and unknown, self and alien (Gilmore, 2003). Monsters are symbols of togetherness.

And now, like Columbus sailing off into the great unknown, I invite you to follow the hero's path, venture out from our known world into dark and unfamiliar territories, confront our imagined fears and engage with the wild things caged in the basement of our psyche. For once we bring into conscious awareness that which is on the edge of consciousness, we kindle a light that illuminates the darkness within, and as every child knows, the best way to deal with a monster is to turn on the light.

REFERENCES

Bawdon F (2009) 'Hoodies or Alter Boys: What is the media stereotyping doing to our British boys?', Women in Journalism report, UK, March 2009.

Bernstein A (2001) *Emotional Vampires*, McGraw-Hill, New York.

Bradshaw J (1988) *Healing the Shame that Binds You*, Health Communications, Deerfield Beach, FL.

Burton P (2012) School based violence and interruption talk at the Centre for Justice and Crime Prevention, Washington, DC.

Byron T (2009a) 'The fear of young people damages us all', *The Telegraph*, London, 17th March 2009.

Byron T (2009b) 'We see children as pestilent', *The Guardian*, 17th March 2009.

Clark C (2011) *Hurt 2.0: Inside the World of Today's Teenagers*, Baker Academics, Michigan.

Davis L & Santos C (2010) *The Monster Imagined*, Inter-Disciplinary Press, Oxford.

Frankel R (1998) *The Adolescent Psyche: Jungian and Winnicottian perspectives*, Routledge, London.

Gilmore D (2003) *Monsters: Evil Beings, Mythical Beasts, and All Manner of Imaginary Terrors*, University of Pennsylvania Press, Philadelphia.

Hillman J (1999) 'The cure of the shadow', Zweig C & Abrams J (eds), *Meeting the Shadow*, Tarcher, New York.

Horney K (1993) *Our Inner Conflicts: A Constructive Theory of Neurosis*, Norton, London (first published 1945).

Jung CG (1973) *Letters*, Vol. 1, Routledge, New York.

Jung CG (1989) *Memories, Dreams, Reflections*, Vintage Books, New York (first published in 1963).

Kearney R (2003) *Strangers, Gods and Monsters: Interpreting Otherness*, Routledge, London.

Lewis Smith V (1995) *Inside the Magic Rectangle*, Gollancz Books, London.

Mansfield H (2006) *Manliness*, Yale University Press, New Haven, CT.

Nelson E (2010) *Creating Humanity, Discovering Monstrosity: Myths and Metaphors of Enduring Evil*, Inter-Disciplinary Press, Oxford.

Richo D (1997) *When Love Meets Fear*, Paulist Press, Mahwah, NJ.

Riley S & Malchiodi C (1999) *Art Therapy with Adolescents*, Jessica Kingsley, London.

Rothman K (2011) 'Hearts of darkness', Heit J (ed), *Essays on Evil in Popular Culture*, McFarland, Jefferson, NC.

Sereny G (1998) *Cries Unheard: The Story of Mary Bell*, Macmillan, London.

Taransaud D (2011) *You Think I'm Evil: Practical Strategies for Working with Aggressive and Challenging Adolescents*, Worth Publishing, London.

Townsend M (2010) 'Teenager-Repellent mosquito must be banned, says Europe', The Observer, London, Sunday 20th June 2010.

Weinstock J (2014) *The Ashgate Encyclopedia of Literary and Cinematic Monsters*, Ashgate Publishing, Surrey.

Yalom I (2002) *The Gift of Therapy: Reflections on Being a Therapist*, Piatkus Books, London.

Speechmark Ⓢ

PART 1

Our unloved and unlived self

SKYGGEN, THE MONSTER OF THE PSYCHE

My devil had been long caged, he came out roaring.

Robert Louis Stevenson

(*Dr Jekyll and Mr Hyde*, 1886, p80)

The Museum of Broken Relationships, founded by two Zagreb artists and former lovers, Olinka Vištica and Drazen Grubišić, showcases a collection of everyday objects left behind at the end of love affairs. The items, donated by people from around the world, are displayed alongside narratives detailing tales of the heartbreak they symbolise. Along with the expected items, such as a teddy bear clutching a heart, a bride's dress, sex toys and pieces of jewellery, are more emotionally charged reminders of loss. There is a dog collar with a red flashing light sent by a man whose wife had killed herself a year after they split up. She had bought it for their little dog who kept wandering off in the dark and getting lost. On a note next to the light, the widower had written: '*I'd said many times during the split that I felt lost and very alone. This little red light has been with me everywhere, in my toilet bag for two years now, killing me every time I see it [...] Please hang it blinking if you use it – it reminds me of a heartbeat. The battery can be replaced*'.

Near the dog collar, there is a large key-shaped bottle opener. It was sent by a young woman after her boyfriend died. On the note she had written: '*You talked to me of love, gave me small gifts every day; this is just one of them. The key to the heart. You turned my head, you just didn't want to sleep with me. I realised how much you loved me only after you died of AIDS*'.

These objects are relics of lost love that we usually shove to the back of a cupboard, never to be seen again. But what is left behind after the breakdown of a relationship cannot always be consigned to a drawer or displayed in a museum. What endures is a collection of internalised beliefs, unfulfilled desires and concealed sorrows that we often repress to distance ourselves from emotional pain. However, we are warned that turning our back on our unloved self is tantamount to inviting untold mischief into our lives, as depicted by the Danish poet and author Hans Christian Andersen in his 1847 story *Skyggen* (The Shadow).

Skyggen, the body of the soul

While visiting the hot southern countries, a courteous and well-mannered scholar and a lover of truth and beauty is struck by the grace of a young woman living in the house opposite. Too shy to approach her himself, he bids his shadow to enter the house across the street in his stead. The Shadow tears itself from its upright master's feet, jumps into the hurly-burly of the narrow streets and slinks through the doorway on the woman's balcony. The young scholar eagerly awaits news of the mysterious maiden, but his shadow does not return to obedience. Confused and embarrassed, he goes back to his northern home where he leads a life of discontented severity. As years and days pass away, he grows more learned and strives to portray a public image of respectability and wisdom, but his health and fortune decline. He writes books about what is true in the world and about what is good and what is beautiful, but no one cares to hear such things; what he says about the truth, and the good, and the beautiful, is, to most people, '*like tossing roses to a cow*' (p230). Resigned to a life of mediocrity, with each passing year, he becomes thinner and thinner, more dreary and ungrateful for everything in his life. Meanwhile, the Shadow, free from bondage and heedless of moral constraints, revels in hedonistic delights that his former master would have condemned as scandalous and morally impermissible. Its uncanny ability to hide in the darkness allows it to peep into humankind's darkest secrets and learn about the evil that lurks in the heart of people, '*what no person should know, but what everyone would like to know*' (p229).

Speechmark

Years later the Shadow calls on his former owner in the guise of a wealthy gentleman dressed in the finest clothes. It has grown fat and prosperous through blackmail and extortion, whereas the scholar, whose years were consumed with philosophical musing, has become poor, frail and shadowlike.

The crafty Shadow offers to employ its old master as its own shadow and promises fortune and healing in return for complete obedience. At first the scholar cannot envision such reversal of roles, but in his dire financial straits, he complies and with wide-eyed naivety agrees to become the Shadow's servant. However, when the Shadow orders him to lie at its feet, as shadows do, the scholar rebels; he refuses to surrender his autonomy and threatens to reveal the truth to the world that the Shadow is but a shadow. But the righteous, learned man is no match for the theatrics and warped ethics of his darker twin.

'*My shadow has gone mad*', the Shadow cries out. '*He thinks he's a human being and that I – just imagine – that I'm his shadow*' (p234).

The unfortunate scholar is swiftly locked away for his own good. In the closing lines of the story, the Shadow delivers him from the little life he has left; as the evening approaches it has its old master secretly executed.

Andersen's tragic and cautionary tale reveals the danger of allowing reason to rule alone, for '*without socialization, passion is a crude barbarian, and without passion, the elegant and polite are dead*' (Nazarian, 2010). The disobedient Shadow embodies all that is hidden and forbidden to its master, all that the law-abiding and well-mannered scholar suppressed in order to enjoy an approving conscience. It personifies not only his lust and greed but also his disowned creative impulses and unrealised potentials. It is his unlived and unloved self caged by pious aspirations, and it is the estranged familiar that longs for restoration.

In Skyggen, as in Jungian psychology, the Shadow is the savage that sleeps within all of us, the Mr Hyde weighed down by societal norm and archaic parental control. It is the '*not me*', all that we regard as inferior and shameful and have repressed in our relentless pursuit of approval. It is the disowned and rejected aspects of our being that remain active within our personal unconscious, and it is the uncanniness that returns upon us at midlife with more unfamiliar pressure.

Forgotten paths

In *Parerga and Paralipomena* (1893), the German philosopher Schopenhauer makes the analogy between the midpoint in the journey of our life and that of a traveller reaching the top of a hill. In our youth, when we are ascending the hill, death is not visible. It lies down at the bottom of the other side. But once we cross the top, death comes into view, and we start the second part of our journey with the same kind of sensation as the criminal experiences with every step on his way to court. Yet, just like the traveller who, on reaching the summit, gets a connected view over the road he has taken and the one ahead, it is when we come to look upon our life as a connected whole that we recognise not only the true relation between all our actions but also that our character and capacities show themselves in their true light. In short, halfway along our journey, the illusions that previously concealed a true view of the world and our selves dissipate, and as the philosopher adds, in the afternoon of life, '*much the same thing happens as at the end of a bal masqué – the masks are taken off*' (p115). We then need to let go, or at least re-evaluate, what has come to define who we are, come to term with the polarities within ourselves and become who we were born to be.

The midlife shadow

Emotional and psychological growth does not end with childhood or when physical maturity is complete. It continues throughout life. Jung emphasises that the task of the second half of life is to let go of our one-sided and outdated youthful bias, rediscover all that is deep within us, reclaim the disowned parts of the self and create a life that has meaning and purpose. In other words, the second half of life is a time for self-actualisation and

psychological enlargement. During this period, all that has been repressed for the benefit of self-marketing, to grant us access to a desired social world or to adapt to the expectations of our early environment and gain the approval of others, pushes for expression and calls for restoration. All that has been dumped in what James Hollis calls the *Swamplands of the Soul* (1996) mutates, spurts and spreads; it gradually draws together and coalesces into a separate 'splinter personality' (Jung, 1951). By midlife, this relatively autonomous entity finds its way to the surface of consciousness and threatens the relative equilibrium of our currently held beliefs.

When confronted with such an unfamiliar and potentially dangerous situation, every cell of our body screams at us to fight or flee that which threatens the foundation of our identity. We might refuse to attune our mind to our years and indulge in the pursuit of immature dreams, cling to a past long gone in a bid to recapture the thrills of juvenile abandon, find temporary respite through elaborate self-deceptions or take comfort in blame and fool ourselves into believing that *evil* is 'over there'.

But fear-based responses do not provide any long-term relief from emotional distress; instead they block out growth and weaken our connections with our selves and those around us. Ultimately all that has been caged demands expression, seeks license and comes out roaring, for '*where we do not go willingly, sooner or later we will be dragged*' (Hollis, 1996, p15). And as Skyggen warns, if everything in us is geared towards one extreme at the expense of the other, we will grow spiritually and emotionally bankrupt, an empty shell that casts no shadow. Conversely, when we embrace the totality of ourselves and tolerate the tension of opposites within our psyche, we kindle a light that illuminates the darkness within.

Turning on the lights

As children we fear the imaginary monsters that live under the bed and hide in the closet, but as the poet points out, '*never has any monster ever heard a battle cry more terrifying than I will turn on a light*' (Koyczan, 2013). We all know that in the light of day, monsters lose their powers; it is only what lurks in the dark that frightens us. Similarly, when we confront our shadow and bring conscious awareness to that which is not the conscious, we shine a light into the darkest corners of our psyche and uncover the alienated parts of our selves that still long for validation – for what is hidden below the surface is what has not been loved.

Engaging with the estranged and forgotten part of our selves can prove to be a slow and painful process, yet it is one of the most important steps towards psychological growth. When we acknowledge and befriend our shadow as a conscious companion, not only does it lessen its destructive power, but it also allows it to become a source of strength that builds our capacity to develop both self-respect and respect for others. For self-awareness is the gateway to choice, creativity and authentic living. It offers not just the option not to act on our immature urges and destructive impulses but the added option to try to let go of them (Goleman, 1996).

Our adolescent shadow

This deep call for wholeness, during which we strive to shift from the old currents that moved us through the first half of life (Kenney, 2007), mirrors the individuation process that takes place in adolescence (see chapter 11). Along with the turbulence that accompanies these transitional stages of development, questions of personal identity emerge together with memories laced with feelings of longing, shame and vulnerability. As Alsford (2006) jokingly remarks, during our adolescence we ask such questions as, '*Who am I and what am I going to do with my life?*', and in our 40s we ask: '*Is this all I am, and what have I done with my life?*'

Not only do we all still carry our teenage self around with us, but it is an enduring component of our psyche. Consequently, it is to be expected that work with adolescents will reawaken emotionally charged memories of our own youth and stir up our unexamined shame. When such unsettling

emotions break free, we run the risk of acting out our own impulses. We must aim to refine these powerful forces, accept them for what they are and acknowledge that something from our own past has found its way in the present. For once we feel more fully understanding of our secret self, we can relate to another person who tries to penetrate that inner territory or threatens that part of us (Zinker, 1978). So, as Frankel remarks, *the work with adolescents also becomes work on ourselves'* (1998, p179).

Conclusion

Although we have some control over our lives, there are unknown forces that exercise considerable power over us. In his book *The Happiness Hypothesis*, social psychologist Jonathan Haidt makes the analogy between a tiny rider perched on the back of an elephant and the interaction between our conscious and unconscious: *'The mind is divided into parts that sometimes conflict. Like a rider on the back of an elephant, the conscious, reasoning part of the mind has only limited control of what the elephant does'* (2006, xi). In other words, in spite of his superior intellectual functioning and strategic reasoning abilities, the rider is no match for the pachyderm that will go more or less where it wants. The same is true of our repressed instinctual urges and primitive desires. These unacknowledged and unloved parts of ourselves operate underground, below the surface of consciousness, where they dictate our behaviour and influence our interactions with others.

Opposing principles exist in all of us; we are both animal and civilised, and psychological wholeness depends not only on an understanding of the conflicting forces within ourselves but also on an acceptance of the un-integrated aspects of the psyche that we regard as immature and shameful. However, developing a more conscious and harmonious relationship with these split of parts is a painful and frightening task. We do not like change, for change implies loss; yet safety in the familiar can be far more costly than authenticity. As Horney emphasises, *'we cannot suppress or eliminate essential parts of ourselves without becoming estranged from ourselves'*

(1945, p111). In short, and as the following case study highlights, to deny entrance to authentic living is to live life on the brink of great shame.

REFERENCES

Alsford M (2006) *Heroes and Villains*, Alsford Darton, Longman & Todd Ltd, London.

Andersen HC (2004) *The Shadow*, published in *Hans Christian Andersen Fairy Tales*. Translated by Tiina Nunnally, Penguin Classics, London.

Frankel R (1998) *The Adolescent Psyche: Jungian and Winnicottian Perspectives*, Routledge, London.

Goleman D (2004) *Emotional Intelligence & Woking with Emotional Intelligence*, Bloomsbury, London (first published in 1996).

Haidt J (2006) *The Happiness Hypothesis: Putting Ancient Wisdom to the Test of Modern Science*, Arrow Books, London.

Hollis J (1996) *Swamplands of the Soul: New Life in Dismal Places*, Inner City Books, Canada.

Horney K (1993) *Our Inner Conflicts: A Constructive Theory of Neurosis*, Norton, London (first published 1945).

Jung C (1991) *Aion: Researches into the Phenomenology of the Self*. Routledge, London (first published in 1951)

Kenney MA (2007) Mysterious Chrysalis: A Phenomenological Study of Personal Transformation. ProQuest, Ann Arbor, MI.

Koyczan S (2013) Turn On the Lights. Performed at NPR's Snap Judgment.

Nazarian V (2010) *The Perpetual Calendar of Inspiration*, Norilana Books, Vermont.

Schopenhauer A (2007) *The Ages of Life*, published in Parerga and Paralipomena: A Collection of Philosophical Essays, Cosimo Classic, New York (first published in 1893).

Stevenson RL (1994) *Dr. Jekyll and Mr. Hyde*, Penguin Classics, London (first published in 1886).

Zinker J (1978) *Creative Process in Gestalt Therapy*, Vintage Books, New York.

Speechmark Ⓢ

AALEYAH'S LONG-LOST TWIN

*Her escape was completely barred; and had every
door in the house been thrown open, she would have felt like a
bird on its first flight from the cage, without a spray
that she dared to rest on.*

Charles Robert Maturin

(*Melmoth the Wanderer*, 1820, p373)

Zayd and Aaleyah's union was not a love story but it grew to be a partnership that created some stability and structure in their lives. When after 20 years of marriage Zayd suddenly died, Aaleyah sank into deep depression and developed an addiction to prescription painkiller. Unable to cope with day-to-day affairs, she moved back in with her parents and started weekly psychotherapy. Two years later she enrolled in a part-time counselling course run by a local nongovernmental organisation in which I regularly taught.

It was near the end of the day when she marched into my office without so much as a knock on the door. She was out of breath, bristling with anger, agitated and on the verge of tears. Her face was flushed and strands of hair had fallen away from her headscarf.

'*She thinks she can get away with anything!*' she shouted.

Aaleyah just had a heated argument with Leah, a lively and confident 21-year-old student whose youthful energy and sometimes undisciplined behaviour often conflicted with Aaleyah's societal dictates.

Her voice was still hoarse from all the yelling. Although she could not remember precisely what had started the argument, she needed an audience to whom she could vent her frustration. She animatedly pointed out numerous times when, according to her, Leah's inconsiderate behaviour was nothing more than an immature bid for attention. She criticised her easy-going and fun-loving attitude, complained about her lack of inhibiting morals and labelled her a self-centred and needy child taking too much group time. Her views were very clear that her unruly young classmate was the epitome of everything that was wrong with the current generation.

When I enquired about her own set of values, Aaleyah defensively replied that rules were there for a reason and stressed that she always followed them. She stated that she was in her 40s and that, unlike her '*immature*' classmate, her behaviour was in accordance with her age. She bragged about her social status and her superior education and claimed she was satisfied with what she had achieved. There was a nervous exuberance in her manners, yet she seemed to be holding something back. Throughout her rant, her eyes were sending signals, as if she were longing for attention but could not directly voice her needs. While I paraphrased what she had said, reflected on what triggered her sudden moral outrage and wondered aloud if there was anything missing in her life, Aaleyah broke eye contact. She sank into her chair, held her head in her hands and quietly sobbed: *'I don't know …* *I'm not made of stone'.* All that she had stuffed away for years burst forth in a flood of tears. It turned out that her interpersonal conflict originated from intrapersonal conflict.

Aaleyah revealed she grew up in a strict hierarchical and patriarchal community that placed great emphasis on obedience, reputation and social status. She recalled that in her teenage years she dreamt of following in the footsteps of her idol, the French designer Gabrielle Bonheur Chanel. Academically and creatively gifted, she graduated with a degree in fashion design. She was offered a scholarship to further her studies but her authoritarian father, who did not support her artistic aspirations, pushed her into an arranged marriage to maintain the family social status. Only a few days before she turned 19, Aaleyah was wed to Zayd, a prosperous businessman 15 years her senior. Zayd, possibly fearing that his young wife's ambition might jeopardise his dominant position as head of the household, reinforced her father's values and demanded she gave up her academic

Speechmark Ⓢ

pursuits. Aaleyah, raised to be a pleaser, complied. She suppressed her creative urges, took to wearing a rigid social mask, kept up appearances at the expense of authenticity and found herself on a very different path from the one she envisioned. Her life was reduced to a monotonous routine. For over two decades her function was confined to supervising household labour, looking after her aging mother-in-law, satisfying her husband's needs in and out of the bedroom and faking happiness.

The inner parental voice

Early social programming, parental expectations and rigid gender paradigms progressively crystallised into rigid patterns of thoughts, beliefs and actions that shielded her from a clear view of herself and the world (Powell, 1969). And like a prisoner who gradually grows attached to her environment, Aaleyah found some sort of safety in her emotional confinement. But her unlived and captive self continued to exist below the surface and, like a slave anxiously yearning for manumission, after the death of her husband, all that she had suppressed rebelled. In searching for some sort of outlet for expression, she found target in Leah who reflected all that she had learned to regard as morally reprehensible. Aaleyah's individuality and creativity had been crushed and ridiculed so relentlessly that she had unconsciously surrendered her autonomy to a shaming and repressive inner critic constantly on guard against violating the family rules. Controlled by rigid parental introjections, she was seeing the world through the eyes of her authoritarian father.

Judy Livingstone defines introjects as '*the internalizations of aspects of the developing child's external interpersonal relationships*' (2004, p26). In other words, we all carry a mini recorder within ourselves which plays, softly but insistently, messages we received in our formative years. The soundtrack of a psychodrama with mother and father singing refrains that begin with '*You should*' and '*You shouldn't*' (Powell, 1969; Ellis, 2011).[8] The inner parental

---

[8] Research estimates that there are around 25,000 hours of these tapes in an average person's head (Bradshaw, 1991).

---

voice is an integral part of all of us, and while it can act as a moral guide and source of comfort, it can also be an unforgiving authority devoid of compassion that many of us tend to question no more than young children would question their parents' authority (Masters, 2013).

Aaleyah's attachment to her parental introjections was such that when Leah's youthful energy triggered her split off parts, the resurgence of intolerable anxieties and intrapsychic conflicts compelled her to re-enact aspects of her negative earlier relationships.

Over time Aaleyah recognised that her lively classmate was not only the embodiment of her unlived and unloved self but also an outer screen onto which she projected powerful impulses that for over two decades had to be denied. She acknowledged that while blame and denial allowed her to maintain the role she adopted to gain the approval of her constrictive environment, it also kept her tied to an anti-developmental alliance with a controlling patriarchal figure that prevented her from having her needs met.

After years spent trapped in a prison without walls, she painfully realised she had outgrown many of her childhood dreams and, with support, she reassessed what had come to define her. She grieved what could no longer be, empathically reconnected with estranged and unloved parts of her self and reclaimed some of her creative energy. And although her internalised parental voice could not always be silenced and still filled her thoughts with shaming and self-depreciating messages, she developed her capacity to take a more positive stance. She learned to answer back to her inner critic with a confidence and grace she never admitted to in her earlier years.

Conclusion

We all know that change is critical to growth, yet we'd rather hold on to what is familiar than venture into unknown territories. As Auden observes, *'we would rather be ruined than changed. We would rather die in our dread*

Speechmark

than climb the cross of the moment and let our illusions die' (1947, p105). But as discussed, to deny entrance to anything that does not comply with our idealised self is to live half a life. It distorts the truth and short-circuits emotional growth, and eventually all that we repress returns with greater determination. As the Jungian psychotherapist Connie Zweig notes, *'the more the shadow hides, the more it's outside awareness, the tighter its hold over us'* (1998).

To ignore the shadow is to be enslaved by powerful unconscious forces. To wage war against it inflames its ferocity; to indulge it narrows our horizons, poisons life and casts a darkness over everything that gives worth to existence. For what hides in the shadow realm is what has not been loved, and what is love-starved gradually grows to monstrous proportions and seeks the illusion of power. It finds targets in others and often constitutes the basis of hatred and prejudice (Bradshaw, 1988).

Our disowned parts are projected in our relationships. We label the attachments of our daily life with shameful traits that are in fact true of ourselves and, like a dog barking at its own reflection, we shun them and fear them for what they reveal to us about ourselves. So blame and fear are nothing but signals by which we can notice what has not been integrated and what still yearns for restoration and validation (Richo, 1997). In other words, before repressed elements of our psyche reach awareness, they often go out into the world. As Bly remarks, *'our psyche in daily life tries to give us a hint of where our shadow lies by picking out people to hate in an irrational way'* (1988, p47).

In his paper on shadow projection and scapegoating, Dempcy (2013) illustrates this point. He recounts a story about when the Swiss psychologist Marie-Louise von Franz first met Carl Jung. Jung asked her to write a list of everything she hated in other people. After she completed her assignment, Jung told von Franz, *'See, that's you! Everything on that list is disavowed parts of yourself'*. The shadow, however, does not only consist of morally reprehensible tendencies, it also displays positive elements that are denied expression (Jung, 1961). So everything we loathe and everything we envy in others is often a pointer as to where our own darkness lurks. As Richo adds, *'every person to whom we react with strong fear, desire, repulsion, or admiration is a twin of our own inner unacknowledged life'* (1999, p5).

Thus, shadow projection is an invaluable tool for self-actualisation and psychological growth. And to explore the rich darkness of our unexamined shame and grant hospitality to the unlived and unloved parts of our self is the first step towards self-respect, compassion, wholeness and authentic living.

REFERENCES

Auden WH (2011) *The Age of Anxiety: A Baroque Eclogue*, Princeton University Press, Princeton, NJ (first published 1947).

Bly R (1988) *The Little Book on the Human Shadow*, Harper Collins, San Francisco, CA.

Bradshaw J (1991) *Taming the Shameful Inner Voice*, published in Meeting the Shadow: The Hidden Power of the Dark Side of Human Nature, Penguin, New York.

Bradshaw J (1988) *Healing the Shame that Binds You*, Health Communications, Deerfield Beach, FL.

Dempcy J (2013) 'Shadow projection and scapegoating in contemporary academic discourse', Published on www.academia.edu.

Ellis GH (2011) *Remembering Frankenstein: Healing the Monster in Every Man*, Author House, Illinois.

Jung C (1989) *Memories, Dreams, Reflections*, Vintage Books, New York (first published in1961).

Livingstone J (2004) 'Dissociation and compulsive eating', published in Journal of Trauma & Dissociation, Vol. 5. USA: The Haworth Press.

Masters RA (2013) *Meeting the Dragon*, R A Masters Publishing, Oregon.

Maturin CR (1998) *Melmoth the Wanderer*, Oxford World's Classics, Oxford (first published in 1820).

Powell J (1969) *Why Am I Afraid to Tell You Who I Am?*, Zondervan, London.

Richo D (1997) *When Love Meets Fear*, Paulist Press, New Jersey.

Richo D (1999) *Shadow Dance*, Shambala Publications, Boston, MA.

Zweig C (1998) Insight and Outlook: an interview with Scott London aired on National Public Radio across the United States and on Radio for Peace International. Produced in California at KCBX.

3

THE UNDERDOG

Lost causes are the only ones worth fighting for.

Jefferson Smith – played by Jimmy Stewart.
(F. Capra. *Mr Smith Goes to Washington*, Columbia Pictures, 1939)

Everybody loves a good underdog story. We cheer for them, scream their names and hope that, despite great adversity and impossible odds, they will turn things around and come out on top. We are wired to hope. We sympathise with those who are unlikely to prevail not only because our sense of justice seeks to rectify an inequitable situation but also because their unexpected victory provides us with the biggest positive emotional pay-off (Vandello, 2007). The Davids versus Goliaths of the world help us believe that we too have the power to overcome self-doubts and to triumph despite the most seemingly overwhelming obstacles. If they can crawl their way upwards, surely so can we. Their hardships resonate with our own personal battles. Their suffering gives meaning to ours. And so perhaps some of us unconsciously reach out to vulnerable youths because they reflect our blind side, and even though we might have lost touch with what lies beneath our social masks, we somehow recognise ourselves in them. Perhaps we are wounded helpers. And may be our rescue missions are motivated by selfish motives and attempts to relieve our own negative states, lessen our unacknowledged despair and satisfy our unresolved infantile emotional needs vicariously through them. Perhaps our career choice was not a choice at all but a *'response to unconscious drives to compensate for childhood experiences of parental impotence, or emotional neglect'* (Johnson, 1991, p318).

Our blind side

We all have a wounded child at the core of our being. It is the orphan of the psyche. It is both a poor motherless thing trying to get our attention and a

juvenile pariah shunned by authority figures. It is a love-starved Oliver Twist who wants 'some more' and a Huckleberry Finn ostracised by polite society. It is an un-parented and mischievous waif who yearns for love, warmth and safety. It is an enduring part of us all that longs to be acknowledged and integrated. Yet when confronted by our unlived and unloved self, rather than engage the otherness within and grant it hospitality, most of us are overcome by fright and many run away (Jung, 1963). We dismiss such encounters' importance and often seek comfort in denial. We sometimes find refuge in ego defence mechanisms and skilfully deceive ourselves with soothing lies to quiet the pain. We push down or edit memories that carry painful emotional weight and look back upon the not-so-good-old-days through a rosy haze of nostalgic reveries.

We instinctively avoid venturing into the obscurity, for we have long been taught that what is pure and good stands in the light, while monsters lurk in the shadow. Our fear of being taken over by all that we have learned to regard as shameful is so great that we'd rather cling to the moral expectations we have internalised and forsake our potential for creative growth than face the painful truth. We are not who we think we are. We are more than a projection made up of other people's projections (Newton, 2011) or a mere collection of internalised beliefs.

We might not wish to know what lies in the darkness, but what lurks in the dark knows about us and, if not acknowledged, it returns in monstrous forms. It gnaws at our capacity for creative living and sabotages our relationships. For the more our disowned self operates outside conscious awareness, the more likely we are to revert to immature ways when our established values are threatened. This is a form of 'emotional hijacking' (Goleman, 1996) in which the sudden resurgence of unprocessed emotional memories blocks off access to the rational mind, prevents clear logical thinking and hinders all possibility for empathic attunement with others. In other words, when knee-deep in emotionally charged situations, the there-and-then intrudes on the here-and-now, and not only are we left trying to deal with the crisis with the limited capabilities of a child, but others become a repository for our own unresolved emotional pain. Of course, as Khan notes, most of us are too conscientious to do such things knowingly, yet we are not 'flawlessly programmed computers; we are imperfect humans, and we give off an assortment of signals of which we can at best be only partly aware' (2001, p79). And so, regardless of our good intentions, we can all succumb to the powerful grip of our own shadow and allow our unresolved pain to get in the way of rational decision making.

Emotionally hijacked – mind the child

We can all appreciate the importance of social masks and how they help us conform to collective expectations and relate with each other, but the real tragedy of life is when these masks, worn too rigidly, turn our lives into performances and hinder our deep-seated needs for nourishing relationships. Frankel (1998) argues that because teenagers are going through the process of individuation (identity formation), they possess an uncanny understanding of the dynamics of revealing and concealing identity. They are skilled experts at detecting fakery and exposing our hidden insecurities, particularly when these are concealed beneath protective layers of aggressive control, excessive sympathy, pride or unconcerned detachment. And thus, when they are on the receiving hand of ambiguous communication, their provocative behaviour can sometimes be nothing more than a wish to crack through our rigidly worn social persona with the secret hope to relate to a more authentic part of us.

Their ability to challenge our personal boundaries and see through our 'as if' personalities can stir up all that festers in the sewage system of the psyche and trigger in us a whole range of fear-based emotional responses. When they upset our fragile psychological equilibrium and threaten our idealised sense of self, vulnerability and authenticity are experienced as a threat and our primitive instincts take over. As Zulueta highlights, 'the greater the threat to our sense of who we feel we are, the more powerful the defense processes

Speechmark Ⓢ

we use' (1993, p124). We might then project onto them what we fear within, avoid or condemn in them what we can't admit in ourselves or depend upon them to provide for what we lack. To satisfy our immature narcissistic needs, compensate for feelings of inadequacy or lessen our negative emotional states, we rescue rather than empower, dictate rather than engage creative thinking, give in to force rather than show emotional vulnerability or shut down our capacity to feel rather than be empathically present.

The greatest burden young people must bear is the unlived lives of the adults in their immediate environment (Jung, 1970). We unconsciously pressure them to carry our own emotional luggage and in the process, despite our wish to bring change, we aggravate what we initially aimed to lessen. The gulf between adolescents and us widens, and their behaviour most assuredly worsens. And once the storm has passed, we often regret the way in which we handled the situation; yet rather than explore our own resistance to contact, we sometimes rationalise in order to justify our initial response, intellectualise to preserve a sense of competency and avoid further emotional meltdown or place the blame on the adolescent's environment. But regardless of our coping strategies, we are often left with a nagging feeling, as Goleman notes, *'the hallmark of such a hijack is that once the moment passes, those so possessed have the sense of not knowing what came over them'* (1996, p14).

Those of us who work with emotionally wounded teenagers pay a great deal of attention to where they come from but very little to where we come from (Zinker, 2001). We often neglect to fully explore our own personal history and the baggage we still carry. Yet, deep beneath our civilised exteriors and social masks lies a world of archaic fears and repressed impulses, and unless we appreciate their true origins, we will act them out. Unless we adopt an open discovering way of being with ourselves and others, our classrooms will turn into theatres where all involved act out their own personal dramas and inner conflicts. As Bly highlights, teachers who have not befriended the conflicting forces within themselves can talk about discipline all day and never get it. But when a teacher has worked with his or her own shadow, *'Students, sense it, and discipline in that room will not be difficult'*. The work an adult does on his or her shadow, Bly adds, results in a *'feeling of natural authority without the authority being demanded'* (1988, p54). So when under the influence of negative emotions or confronted with intimidation, manipulation, resistance or efforts at seduction, the only way to break the cycle of hate and hurt is to pause, ask of ourselves how we may have consciously or unconsciously contributed to the situation and wonder what it is that we are trying to gain or to hide. As Jung judiciously points out, *'if there is anything that we wish to change in the child, we should first examine it and see whether it is not something that could better be changed in ourselves'* (1939, p285).

Conclusion

Young people whose realities have been impacted by early failures in attunement are not the only ones who need to defend against shame-based memories. For example, many of us working in the caring professions often protect ourselves from similar anxieties by enacting the role of the compulsive carer (Zulueta, 1993). But no matter how disguised they are, our attempts to satisfy personal unmet needs will only succeed if the other is willing to cooperate. And it is unlikely that adolescents who have been hurt by the people who were supposed to look after them will welcome our offers of help and support with open arms. This in turn might elicit a deep sense of helplessness in ourselves.

Self-deceit and lack of awareness are forces that promote fear, intolerance and conflicts. Conversely, an empathic exploration of our shadow elements fosters the building of meaningful working alliances. As the old adage points out, charity often begins at home; in developing understanding for our own unloved self, we are also in the process of deepening our compassion for others. We need to be honest with ourselves before we can risk honest communication with others. But that kind of psychological change does not occur through rational processes; to grant hospitality to the estranged and forgotten part of our selves is not an intellectual endeavour. We cannot think

Speechmark

ourselves out of difficult emotions. Instead we have to stay present with the feelings triggered inside of us … and pause … and allow ourselves to be comfortable with being uncomfortable. Regardless of how hard we try, we cannot escape from what is within, but we can sit with it as we would sit with a young child and ask him what he wants us to know, listen to what he answers and be open to learning from him. For only once we have mothered our own wounded self will we be able to provide others with the parenting they never received. Furthermore, as the next case study demonstrates, to befriend the otherness within and learn to live with it in tight harmony not only lessens its destructive power but also allows us to communicate to others that impulsive urges and shame-based memories can be survived rather than acted out. As Storr (1989) emphasises, only a person who has known and faced despair within him- or herself can convey to others that despair can be overcome.

REFERENCES

Bly R (1988) *A Little Book on the Human Shadow*, Harper Collins, New York.

Capra F (1939) *Mr. Smith Goes to Washington*, Columbia Pictures, Culver City, CA.

Frankel R (1998) *The Adolescent Psyche: Jungian and Winnicottian Perspectives*, Routledge, London.

Goleman D (1996) *Emotional Intelligence*, Bloomsbury, London.

Johnson WD (1991) Predisposition to Emotional Distress and Psychiatric Illness among Doctors: the role of unconscious and experiential factors, published in The British Journal of Medical Psychology, Vol. 64. Wiley-Blackwell, UK.

Jung CG (1939) *The Integration of the Personality*, Farrar & Rinehart, New York.

Jung CG (1970) *Psychological Reflections*, Princeton University Press, Princeton, NJ.

Jung C (1989) *Memories, Dreams, Reflections*, Vintage Books, New York (first published in 1963).

Khan M (2001) *Between Therapist and Client, the New Relationship* (revised edition), Holt Paperbacks, New York.

Newton T (2011) *Embracing Otherness*, TEDGlobal Talk, Edinburgh.

Storr A (1989) *Churchill's Black Dog*, HarperCollins, London.

Vandello J (2007) *The Appeal of the Underdog*, published in Personality and Social Psychology Bulletin, Vol. 33. Sage Publications, New York.

Zinker J (2001) *Sketches: An Anthology of Essays, Art, and Poetry*, The Gestalt Press, Cambridge.

Zulueta de F (1993) *From Pain to Violence: The Destructive Roots of Destructiveness*, Whurr Publishing, London.

Speechmark

4

SAM, THE CYBERSPACE JUNKIE

*I have a sadness shield that keeps out all the sadness,
and it's big enough for all of us.*

Max – played by Max Records
(Spike Jonze. *Where the Wild Things Are*, Warner Bros, 2009)

Sam was the kind of teenager the tabloids regularly label '*feral*', and for the first time in my professional life, the advice from W. C. Fields, '*don't work with children or animals*', made complete sense. Like many of the young people I work with, Sam grew up in a violent home. His world came crashing down when at five years old his mother who had always stood between him and his father's impatience was diagnosed with lung cancer; she died within six weeks. Three years later Sam's father married a woman who demanded he choose between her and his son. He chose her, and Sam was sent to live with his mother's sister. After a childhood devastated by loss and violence and years spent in a reality that forbade autonomy, Sam had shut down and escaped into a virtual world. He became a cyberspace junkie who spent countless hours locked in computer-generated environments, and his plugged-in life was much richer than his real life. By day he was an Oliver Twist lookalike, a pale and thin 14-year-old boy with sandy hair and a ready fake smile that never managed to fully hide the sadness in his eyes. But by night Sam was a force to be reckoned with. He transformed into a mighty hero who engaged in hand-to-hand combat with battle-hardened warriors; he turned into a cybernetically enhanced supersoldier and a sworn protector of the universe. By night Sam was the master of his own universe.

His immersion in virtual realities and identification with indestructible fictional characters seemed to answer a deep psychological need, his need to be in control, to put on a powerful persona to compensate for the lack of warmth and safety in his life and conquer his childhood fears. Sam's

Speechmark (S)

hostile early environment and the lack of affect-regulative interactions had interfered with his social and emotional development led to a negative world view and compromised his ability to form safe and secure attachment bonds. So by locking himself in this dreamlike imitation of life, Sam somehow managed to remain connected with the world while simultaneously hiding from it.

Game on/over

Sam and I had been working together for nearly two months. The work was unrewarding and I had already convinced myself that he was beyond help. When we first met, he mentioned his mother and briefly shared his experience of growing up with domestic violence. He spoke without sadness or anger, in a flat and monotone voice, like a machine imbued with the ability to mimic human speech but unable to convey emotions. Sam's emotional vacuity was contagious. His recount of abandonment left me cold, detached and unsympathetic. In the subsequent sessions, any attempt on my part to connect with him was met with greater resistance, hostility and contempt. When Sam was not employing all his skills and creativity to ridicule me, confirm my insecurities, provoke a fight or remind me that I was nothing but a '*middle-class wanker*' who'd '*never get it*', he'd shut down, ignore me and spend his weekly sessions playing games on his phone, updating his Facebook status or browsing YouTube for the latest '*happy slap*' attack videos from the neighbourhood. In spite of my constant efforts, Sam had a more intimate relationship with his mobile phone than he did with me. I had silently labelled him a lost cause and often felt like giving up on him. Our relationship was that of an '*uninvolved parent and unseen child*' (Davies & Frawley, 1994).

Needless to say, Sam's contemptuous behaviour challenged my professional competence. I often felt deskilled and frustrated, and even though it had the potential to be counter-therapeutic, I regularly wanted to intervene more directly to shake him out of his frozen state.

Me: *Sometimes it feels to me like you have a lot on your mind. Things you don't want to share.*

Sam: *And?*

Me: *And sometimes I really struggle. I feel some of your pain, and I feel very alone with it.*

Sam: *That's your fucking problem!*

My feelings of frustration grew to murderous rage; I felt an overwhelming urge to teach him a lesson. Yet Sam was right, it was partly my problem. His behaviour had reawakened my fears of rejection and my unresolved infantile dependency needs. But I lacked both the robustness to tolerate the emotional onslaught and the necessary insight to recognise that my blocks and his resistance were intertwined and fed of one another. So, to relieve my own negative states and preserve a sense of competency, rather than show emotional vulnerability, I opted for an uncharacteristically domineering attitude. Armoured with an emotional force field and a good dose of bravado I went back for the kill. And I wanted him to go down.

Me: *What I am trying to say is that sometimes we all feel pain and sometimes we feel so much pain that we don't want to feel anything anymore.*

It was not so much what I said, but how I said it. As I am writing these words I recall the way I stood: head back, arms crossed, with a winning smile and an air of smug confidence. As if I were gloating, I thought, '*I'm smarter than you are and I can smash through your defences*'. Like most children who have experienced threatening environments, Sam was finely attuned to non-verbal emotional communication (Jones, 2003). He saw right through me. Our relationship was about to switch from an '*uninvolved parent and unseen child*' position to an '*impulsive abuser and helpless victim*' drama (Davies & Frawley, 1994).

Suddenly the atmosphere in the room shifted. Detachment and complacent inertia transformed into blame and chaos. Sam stood up and stared at me with a fixed predatory gaze, eyebrows scrunched together; enraged like a cornered beast, he kicked a chair and with a come-on-fight-me look in his eyes threatened to '*beat the living shit*' out of me. My cheeks were burning. I could hear the thumping of my heart and feel my lungs kicking at my chest. My body was on high alert, ready to release the fight-or-flight response. But I remained still, flushed and frozen like a deer in the headlights. I was petrified. Before I had time to collect myself, Sam stormed out of the room, leaving me shaken, rejected, shamed and on the verge of tears. I had unconsciously urged what I had naively hoped to lessen.

Then it hit me like a left hook from Smokin' Joe Frazier that Sam and I were relying on similar coping mechanisms and my own resistance had triggered his aggressive response.

Reflection

Sam's avoidance to forming a working alliance was both a re-enactment of earlier modes of interpersonal relations and a form of communication. It was his way to convey how he was made to feel and how he managed to survive when his basic needs for love and empathic attunement were not met; when unable to physically fight his way out of the situation or run away from his hostile environment, the only choice was to freeze and cast off his relational needs. Yet, even though the utter helplessness and detachment I experienced somehow mirrored the way in which Sam felt and how he dealt with the situation, there was more to it. His behaviour had reawakened painful elements of my personal history, and my reluctance to explore my own negative attachment experiences was partly the reason why his resistance to contact was so fierce.

Provocative behaviour is often how emotionally wounded teenagers express what words cannot convey, the shame and the fear they endured in their

Speechmark Ⓢ

formative years. As Wieland (1998) remarks, if we only interpret their challenging behaviour as wilful defiance and ignore what they have triggered in us, not only do we miss opportunities to gain a deeper understanding of our own inner life and explore their early dynamics, but we also fail to provide them with healthier responses than the ones they experienced. And of greater consequence, we risk re-enacting aspects of their early relationships and in the process confirm their negative world view.

Adolescents, and particularly those who have endured adverse childhood experiences, will force us to face all that we have repressed, ostracised and disowned and all that which has not had the chance to mature. So, as Allen (2001) suggests, we must seek points of connection and work on issues mirrored to us by the young person in order to expand our own consciousness and be of greater service to the adolescent. But this is not something we can do alone. Peer and supervisory support can provide us with a space to reconnect with the estranged parts of our selves so that we can learn to untangle what belongs to others and what belongs to us and adopt the empathetic presence necessary to respond flexibly to external stimuli and internal states (*we will further explore the need for peer support in the following two chapters*).

Restart and reset

I was not sure if Sam would ever return. He did. A week later, right on time, he kicked the door open, walked in my office with a devil-may-care swagger, put his bag down and stood with his back resting against the front door. He stood motionless, silent, eyes cast downwards, his clenched fists deep in his coat pockets. Everything about him screamed: '*I'm not in the mood, don't mess with me*'. I remained in silence with him. After minutes that felt like hours, he allowed his eyes to meet mine. I ventured a timid '*Hi*'. He did not reply. I leant slightly towards him and clumsily stated the obvious.

Me: *I guess you don't want to talk today, and it's okay.*

Speechmark

Sam folded his arms. His mouth fell open and his brows lifted in mock surprise. My heart started racing. Again I felt powerless, impotent and rejected. For the second time, I felt myself coming to the point of wanting to transform into a domineering authority figure. On the one hand, I felt the urge to push back, to speak my mind and to commit mindless violence in a desperate attempt to preserve a sense of control. On the other hand, I wanted to rescue him, to quickly take both of us out of this lonely place. That boy was clearly an expert at putting me back in touch with my own untended wounds and rattling the skeletons in my closet. I paused and waited for the impulse to fade so that rather than defend against disruptive emotions I could use them as guides to access Sam's inner world of perception while remaining in touch with my own experiences.

I described what was happening between us and voiced the impact it had on me hoping he'd then be able to acknowledge and explore his own feelings as they arose in me. For to help others to accept and open themselves, not only do we need to accept and reveal ourselves to them, but we also need to stay in the process and take some risks in the co-creation of experience, understanding and knowledge (Finley & Evans, 2009).

Me: *You seem to be miles away and I'm struggling to give you my full attention. I can see you with my eyes. You are at a hand's distance away, yet I can't reach you, and I feel … I feel very alone … I feel helpless … I feel powerless.*

Sam rolled his eyes and let out an exasperated sigh.

Me: *And this is really not working for me. I want to hide my feelings. I don't want you to see me like that, but I also want to be honest with you … I feel so powerless that there's a part of me that wants to grab you by the shoulders and shake you. I mean really shake you back and forth … but I am not going to do that. I wouldn't do that to you. I'm just thinking aloud.*

Thinking aloud is a way to model self-reflection to help children and adolescents articulate and monitor their internal conflicts and urges rather than act upon them. As Powell notes, '*we either speak out our feelings or we will act them out*' (1969, p44).

Sam looked up. The atmosphere in the room lightened.

> Me: *I think it's normal to want to shake others when we feel alone, when we're hurting inside.*

My response contradicted his negative expectations. Sam's eyes were wide open and he was looking at me with a steady gaze. To allow him to reflect upon his own affective state, I continued disclosing my emotional responses and sharing the different strategies I wanted to use to compensate for my feelings of helplessness.

> Me: *And you know, there's another part of me that wants to walk up to you and put my arms around you … and hug you really tight … and tell you that everything will work out … tell you that I'm here for you and that no matter what happens, I'll be there for you … I think that this part of me wants to take the both of us away from that lonely place … I know it's a hurting place.*

We stayed in silence for a short while. This time, the space between us was filled with a fragile intimacy and renewed hope. We were deepening our abilities to be vulnerably engaged with each other while respecting our own unique ways of being in the world. We were learning to stay in the moment and be both comfortable with being uncomfortable with each other.

> Me: *But I won't do that either. You don't need rescuing and I don't want to take your power away. I believe you're strong enough and creative enough to find your own way out … Yet I guess it's normal to want to attack or take people's power when we feel powerless.*

There was a sadness in his eyes. I felt it too and allowed him to see the hurt in mine. It was unusual for Sam to be with someone willing to venture into his reality and hurt with him. This was a form of empathic imagination, a process defined not by the ability to feel for someone who is in pain but by the ability to feel with the other (Wilson, 2012) so that the sufferer can explore his feelings as they take place within an empathic other.

Me: *And yet there's another part of me that wants to ignore you back so that you'd understand what I'm feeling inside … so that I won't be alone with the pain … but I guess you already know what it feels like to be ignored.*

I paused so that we could reflect on what was happening between us, understand how we had both relied on similar coping strategies and reconnect with our own individuality.

Me: *I'm wondering if sometimes you also try to tell me things, you know, without using words?*

Sam nodded.

Me: *Thank you. I feel less alone now. I feel safe. Is it the same for you?*

Tolerating my affective states while containing those of Sam and empathically mirroring them back to him encouraged reciprocal engagement. Sam grabbed a game of Jenga. He set up the wooden blocks and silently invited me to join him in a game. He had found his own way to move beyond the resistance. We spent the rest of our session playing. And every time the Jenga tower collapsed, we carefully built it back up, one block at a time, symbolically and playfully re-enacting what had happened between us. And so, together we learned that we can only achieve a sense of self in collaboration with others. Just as every wooden block supports and builds

upon others, we are all involved in facilitating, or preventing, each other's process of coming more fully into the world, a process that, as Zinker notes, involves '*exchanges of energy which stimulate and nourish the other but do not deplete one's own vitality and power*' (2001, p39).

Our subsequent meetings were filled with both structured and spontaneous games, improvised imaginative play and art activities during which the both of us experimented with new approaches, enhanced our capacity for creative thinking and built a healthier relational space conducive to growth and more positive patterns of relating.

Conclusion

Behaviour is a form of communication, and as far as challenging adolescents are concerned, their actions speak much louder than words. Their disruptive behaviour often arises from a state of unconscious fear. As Forbes and Post put it, '*scared children do scary things*' (2009, p4). This delayed reaction to the hurt they experienced in their formative years will at times resonate with our own painful attachment history. If we remain unaware of these powerful forces, not only will we experience vulnerability as a threat, but we are also likely to re-enact the disorganised dynamics of our earlier years in our present relationships. In short, without awareness, we have no choice.

When working with vulnerable young people, our most valuable resource is our own self. Unless we reconnect with all that is hiding underneath ego, awareness and integrate it into an enlarged self-concept, unprocessed emotional memories and early terrors will infect our present and anticipated future with past anguish. And, as we will explore in the following two chapters, to reclaim all that is deep within us and provide ourselves with all that we have been denied is not a solitary endeavour; it is a long and arduous venture that can only be undertaken in the presence of a caring other.

REFERENCES

Allen P (2001) 'Art making as spiritual path', Rubin JA (ed), *Approaches to Art Therapy: Theory and technique*, 2nd edn, Brunner-Routledge, Philadelphia, PA.

Davies J & Frawley M (1994) *Treating the Adult Survivor of Childhood Sexual Abuse*, Basic Books, New York.

Finley L & Evans K (2009) *Relational-Centred Research for Psychotherapists: Exploring Meanings and Experience*, Wiley-Blackwell, West Sussex.

Forbes H & Post B (2009) *Beyond Consequences, Logic, and Control: A Love-Based Approach to Helping Children with Severe Behaviours*, Beyond Consequences Institute, Boulder, CO.

Jones D (2003) *Communicating with Vulnerable Children*, Gaskell, London.

Jonze S (2009) *Where the Wild Things Are*, Warner Bros, Burbank, CA.

Powell J (1969) *Why Am I Afraid to Tell You Who I Am?*, Zondervan, London.

Wieland S (1998) *Techniques and Issues in Abuse-Focused Therapy with Children and Adolescents: Addressing the Internal Trauma*, Sage Publications, Thousand Oaks, CA.

Wilson EG (2012) *Everyone Loves a Good Train Wreck: Why We Can't Look Away*, Sarah Crichton Books, New York.

Zinker J (2001) *Sketches: An Anthology of Essays, Art, and Poetry*, The Gestalt Press, Cambridge.

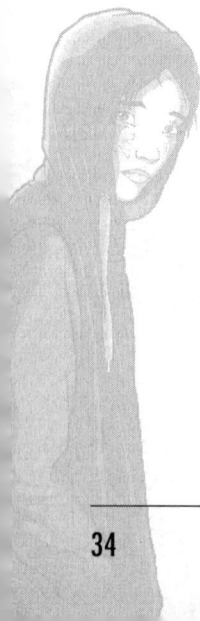

5

OUR FEARS, THE GHOSTS OF CHRISTMAS PAST

Sometimes, reaching out and taking someone's hand is the beginning of a journey. At other times, it is allowing another to take yours.

Vera Nazarian

(*The Perpetual Calendar of Inspiration*, 2010)

New York comedian Jerry Seinfeld observed that when at a funeral, most of us would be better off in the casket than delivering the eulogy. His statement hints at a survey which suggests that most of us fear public speaking (*glossophobia*) more than we fear death (*thanatophobia*). The study conducted in 1973 asked more than 2,500 people to list their greatest fears; speaking before a group topped the list, well ahead of dying. The survey, published in the 7 October 1973 issue of *The Sunday Times* and later in *The Book of Lists* (Wallechinsky & Wallace, 1977), reports the top 10 human fears as follows:

1-	Public Speaking	41%
2-	Heights	32%
3-	Insects and Bugs	22%
4-	Financial Difficulties	22%
5-	Deep Water	21%
6-	Illness	19%
7-	Death	19%
8-	Flying	18%
9-	Loneliness	14%
10-	Dogs	11%

Although this list is now out of date, because new phobias such as terrorist attacks have since appeared, recent studies confirm that public speaking still strikes fear into the hearts of many of us. In 2014, it was number three in the list of things that most scared Brits.[9] Yet developmental studies suggest that we are born with only two instinctual fears: loud noises and falling (Murphy, 2007). As demonstrated in the infamous and highly controversial 'Little Albert Experiment' (1920), our fear reactions, apart from those created by the sudden removal of support or loud sound, are conditioned emotional responses.

Little Albert

In 1920, behaviourist John Broadus Watson, along with his graduate student-turned-wife, Rosalie Alberta Rayner, presented 11-month-old-baby Albert with the stimuli of a friendly white rat and observed his reactions. The animal did not provoke fear in Albert but inspired curiosity. In later trials, every time the child reached for the playful rodent, Watson and Rainer frightened him by striking a hammer upon a suspended steel pipe. The sharp clanging sound startled little Albert and caused him to fall forward and cry. After repeated pairing of the two stimuli, not only was the sight of the rat alone enough to cause Albert to crawl away in fear, but his anxiety response had generalised to visually similar objects. Whenever he was presented with other furry stimuli, such as a fur coat or a teddy bear, his lips puckered and trembled; he whimpered and then burst into tears (Watson, 1923). This conditioned fear persisted. Over a year later, familiar objects that shared the same characteristics as a white rat still evoked negative responses. The part of Albert's developing brain responsible for registering emotions and detecting threat had been imprinted with the following message: anything that is furry is dangerous.[10]

---

[9] https://yougov.co.uk/news/2014/03/20/afraid-heights-not-alone.

[10] **Finding Little Albert.** In 2010 a group of researchers studying the long-term effects of conditioned fear, tracked down what happened to little Albert. Their seven-year quest led them to a small graveyard in Maryland, USA. Albert, whose real name was Douglas Merritte, died in May 1925, at the age of six after contracting hydrocephalus: a build-up of fluid on the brain. The inscription on the little gravestone read: '*The sunbeam smile, the zephyr's breath, all that it knew from birth to death.*'

As Watson and Rainer cruelly demonstrated, most of our fears are learned responses, and they exist in relation to something else. To put it another way, what we fear in the present is something that was only dangerous in the past: *'we are still afraid of what is no longer really fearsome'* (Richo, 1997, p23). And so, it stands to reason that stage fright is linked to the fear of failure and the fear to be heckled, rejected and exposed as the imperfect beings we believe ourselves to be. A fear that can be traced back to infantile anxieties, times when something necessary for our emotional well-being was missing, when our caregivers were unavailable or unable to provide for our needs and when our fearful affects were not adequately regulated.

Running away from oneself

We all long to be fully seen, met and understood. We instinctively seek connections. Not only do we come into the world pre-wired for loving attachment, but nourishing relationships create a positive feedback loop of social, emotional and physical well-being (Seppala, 2012). As the saying goes, together we thrive, alone we strive. We are social animals, and connectedness and interdependence is what gives purpose and meaning to our existence (Waal de, 2005). We live, we breathe and we die for love. But for genuine relationships to happen and for love to grow, we first have to allow our most vulnerable and authentic self to be truly seen (Brown, 2010), and that's where most of us struggle. In spite of our innate predisposition for emotional bonding, when it comes to giving or receiving love we all have so many fears that often, we'd rather hide behind comforting yet outmoded coping mechanisms than let ourselves be vulnerably seen. As discussed in chapter 1, unprocessed emotional memories remain in the psyche, and they nurture falsehood and destroy hope. This *'historical dressing up of real life situations'* (Ferenczi, 1955, p259) poisons the truth of who we are, prevents us from giving of our true self, interferes with the possibility of having our needs met and ultimately sabotages our relationships. Consider this short tale of heartbreak and shame-induced fear.

Theo was a middle-aged, hardened bachelor who sought safety in impersonal interactions devoid of emotional depths or intimacy. He was fond of saying that love was the only mental disorder not listed in the DSM V (*Diagnostic and Statistical Manual of Mental Disorders*) and that at least with mental illnesses you don't have to buy flowers for the *thing* making you ill. Theo had lost both his parents at an early age and had been brought up by his maternal grandmother, a well-meaning but overly protective woman who allowed him little autonomy and involved herself in every aspect of his life. The lack of personal space and the losses he suffered had led to a fear of both abandonment and engulfment that kept him locked in an endless merry-go-round of temporary and unfulfilling affairs. Theo had spent his adult life stuck in a continuous rebound cycle searching for that warm feeling of worth he once experienced, yet the defences he had built to protect from both loss and unwanted intrusion denied him the very thing he sought. Until the day he unexpectedly lowered his guards. The young woman he'd just been introduced to shook his hand and smiled for a little longer than expected. His heart thudded in his chest, and that was the precise moment when Theo fell. And he fell hard. Overpowered by the giddy euphoria that comes to all middle-aged men going through their first adolescent love, Theo spent the subsequent two weeks with a childlike smile on his face. Not knowing what to do with his *young* feelings, he wrote and sent love poems and allowed himself to trust in the unknown and love without boundaries. But as the possibility for a nourishing and intimate relationship became increasingly real, old fears resurfaced. Only a fortnight after his encounter, in the quiet of night when all that hides in the shadow realm is most active, a nagging little inner voice broke the silence. At first it was a whisper: '*If I were you I would not wear my heart on my sleeve … and what exactly made you think it was a good idea to write love poems to someone you've just met?*'. Then it grew louder: '*You are a fool! Do you want to get hurt again?*'. And louder: '*You'd better hide your vulnerability. Hide it with contempt, hide it with pride, anger or humour, but hide it*'. Overpowered by archaic fears, Theo picked up his phone and abruptly ended the relationship.

Fear is innate in every living thing, and it serves preservation. When confronted with danger, the fight-or-flight response automatically kicks in and overrides the reasoning part of the brain that governs social control, encourages rational thinking and manages other higher-order executive functions.[11] Although the fight-or-flight strategy can be an effective survival method when confronted with external danger (after all, it kept our ancestors from becoming the sabre-toothed tiger's dinner), we cannot physically defeat, nor can we escape, what's within. When we deny our fears or try to run away from them, they increase and metastasise into something worse (Tutu, 2010), something that eventually impedes reflective functioning and weakens our connections with ourselves and others. Conversely, when we cultivate compassion for our self and lay claim to what hides within, we no longer need fear it occurring outside our control (Kopp, 1991).

Re-membering the broken self

When it comes to relationships, a lot of our fears originate from a lack of safety. They can be traced back to the helplessness many of us experienced in the face of an environment that at times failed to provide the support we needed as infants (Guntrip, 1969). They belong to the un-parented and affection-starved child in all of us who still longs for a loving and consistent caregiver. To put it another way, like Dickens's Ghost of Christmas Past, they are signals reminding us that the exiled parts of our self, caged in the basement of the psyche, need to be integrated so that we can be whole once again.

Wilson (2006) notes that the descent into the cellar of the unconscious is analogous to the ascent of the soul. Although they appear to move in opposite directions, they both reach the same end. He writes: '*Both travel from visible to invisible, outside to inside, known to mysterious*' (2006, p4).

---

[11] For example, since the 9/11 terror attack on the World Trade Centre, the word 'terrorism' evokes such fear that many of us are now willing to spend more on flight insurances that only cover 'death-by-terrorism' than on cheaper insurances that cover 'death-by-any-cause' (*Newsweek*, 2007).

Speechmark

The way up, Wilson adds, is the same as the way down. So in order to move forward, we need to retrace our steps back to where things went wrong and reclaim all that is deep within us. But to find our way back to what was once known and has since been forgotten and provide ourselves with all that we have been denied but still long for is a painful journey that very few of us can make on our own. As Adams's modern interpretation of the 2,000-year-old Indian folk tale 'A Flowering Tree' highlights, to restore wholeness to a fragmented body, not only do we need to *re*-member the split-off parts of our self, but we also need to remember them in the company of an empathic and accepting witness. In short, the past can only become the past once we have put it behind in the here-and-now and most importantly in the presence of a caring other. One of the rationales behind the need for a sensitive and empathic other rests upon the fact that memory is altered every time it is accessed, and the change depends upon the individual physical and psychological state at the time of remembering. This implies that when a painful event is remembered within a safe environment and in the presence of a compassionate other, the memory will gradually become less painful (Philippson, 2001).

A Flowering Tree (Adams, 2008)

Kumudha was a young and beautiful village girl bestowed with the magical power to transform into a blossoming tree. The ritual required two pitchers of the clearest water, one to change Kumudha into a tree, from which she and her sister gathered fragrant flowers which they sold at the royal palace, and the other to return her to human form. During one of her transformations, Kumudha caught the attention of the king's son who, bewitched by both her beauty and powers, asked for her hand in marriage. They fell deeply in love and were wed a few days later, and every night, while the great city slept, '*together they spread out the flowers […] and made love amongst the delicate scents*' (2008, p17). But the prince's younger sister was jealous of Kumudha's magical gift. While her brother was away hunting, she took the princess to the royal orchard and demanded she performed the ritual

for a group of her friends. After Kumudha turned into the blossoming tree, they broke her branches, tore off her flowers, carelessly spilled the pitchers of water and abandoned her in mid-metamorphosis. When she returned to human form, Kumudha was reduced to a shapeless stump of flesh, a hideous freak neither tree nor woman. She whimpered in shame and crawled into a gutter. From then on, she lived on the street, slept with animals and begged for her food. Days and months passed before she was rescued by a band of minstrels who included her in their travelling freak show. Meanwhile, distraught at his wife's disappearance, the heartsick prince renounced worldly possessions and wandered throughout the kingdom in search of his beloved. His journey took him to a far-off town where a popular travelling circus featuring the monstrous Tree-Woman was set up. Although Kumudha and the prince had spent many years apart, they immediately recognised each other.

'*Quick! Get two pitchers of the clearest water*', murmured the Tree-Woman. '*Pour water over me and I shall be a tree again. Where my branches are broken, set them right. Where a leaf has been damaged, bind it up. And when my wounds are healed, pour water from the second pitcher and I, Kumudha, will be whole again*'. And so, the prince and Kumudha returned to the moment where things went wrong. He helped her confront her traumatic past and piece together her broken self. After the prince performed the loving ritual and Kumudha was restored to her human form, they held each other tightly and their love blossomed anew.

Conclusion

In his remarkable autobiographical book *Man's Search for Meaning*, Jewish psychiatrist and Holocaust survivor Frankl suggests, '*live as if you were living already for the second time and as if you had acted the first time as wrongly as you are about to act now*' (1946, p114). In other words, let's imagine that the present is past and that the past may yet be changed so that we may return to a more authentic, compassionate and creative way of living. But as the above folk tale and the following case study emphasise, confronting painful reminders and piecing together a broken self is an arduous journey that not only requires a process of remembering but also the presence of a fellow traveller willing to make a journey similar to ours. The wounded and disowned aspects of our self cannot be addressed and reintegrated until they come to exist affectively in the mind of an empathic witness, because the experience of sharing our inner selves with a caring and consistent other is often what we have been missing all our lives (Bromberg, 2006; Friel & Friel, 1991). In other words, psychological wholeness can be restored only through reflective mirroring and empathic attunement.

REFERENCES

Adams J (2008) *A Flowering Tree* (Audio CD), Warner Music Group – Nonesuch, New York.

Beck H (2009) 'Finding little albert,' Washington: American Psychologist; Vol. 64, No. 7; October 2009.

Begley S (2007) 'The roots of fear', published in *NewsWeek*. New York: 24 December 2007.

Bromberg P (2006) *Awakening the Dreamer: Clinical Journeys*, The Analytic Press, Mahwah, NJ.

Brown B (2010) *The Gift of Imperfection*, Hazelden Information & Educational Services, Center City, MN.

Ferenczi S (1994) *Final Contributions to the Problems and Methods of Psycho-analysis*, Karnac Books, London (first published in 1955).

Frankl V (2004) *Man's Search for Meaning*, Rider, London (first published in 1946).

Friel J & Friel L (1991) *Adult Children: The Secrets of Dysfunctional Families*, Health Communications Inc, Deerfield Beach, FL.

Guntrip H (1969) *Schizoid Phenomena: Object Relations and the Self*, Hogarth Press, London.

Kopp S (1991) *Tale of a Descent into Hell*, published in Meeting The Shadow: The Hidden Power of the Dark Side of Human Nature, Penguin, New York.

Murphy J (2007) *The Power of your Subconscious Mind*, Wilder Publications, Virginia, MN.

Nazarian V (2010) *The Perpetual Calendar of Inspiration*, Norilana Books, Vermont.

Philippson P (2001) *Self in Relation*, The Gestalt Journal Press, New York.

Richo D (1997) *When Love Meets Fear*, Paulist Press, Mahwah, NJ.

Seppala E (2012) 'Connect to thrive', published in *Psychology Today*. New York: Sussex Publishers; August 2012.

Tutu DM (2010) *Made for Goodness: And Why This Makes All the Difference*, Rider, London.

Waal de F (2005) *Our Inner Ape: The Best and Worst of Human Nature*, Granta Books, London.

Wallechinsky A & Wallace D (2004) *The Book of Lists*, Canongate Books, Edinburgh (first published in 1977).

Watson J (1923) *Experimental Investigation of Babies*, Stoelting Co, Wood Dale, IL.

Watson P (1973) What People Usually Fear. London: The Sunday Times; 7th October 1973.

Wilson E (2006) *The Melancholy Android: On the Psychology of Sacred Machines*, State University of New York Press, New York.

6

THE ICE MAIDEN

I desire the company of a man who could sympathise with me; whose eyes would reply to mine.

Marie Wollstonecraft Shelley

(*Frankenstein or the Modern Prometheus*, 1818, p16)

Margaret was a psychotherapist in her late 50s with many years of experience working within a psychodynamic tradition. She never showed any emotion, rarely smiled and acted as a blank canvas onto which her clients could project personal thoughts, feelings and experiences about themselves and significant others. While most of Margaret's patients experienced her as a skilled and attentive listener, Scott had labelled her 'The Ice Maiden' and often remarked that her silent, empathic head-nodding reminded him of those plastic nodding dogs on car dashboards.

Scott was a short-tempered 20-year-old university student struggling with depressive symptoms. He had been brought up by a financially successful but intimacy-incompetent father and a cold and withholding mother. From very early on he learned that 'grown men don't cry' and feelings of any kind were disruptive and therefore best kept hidden. Scott followed in the footsteps of his parents and became a socially inept emotional recluse alienated from life and love.

Margaret and Scott had been working together for over six months and not much had changed. Their weekly sessions were often filled with superficial material and long silences that echoed the dynamics played out in Scott's early environment. Margaret's neutral demeanour and detached engagement made Scott feel right *at home* and allowed him to hold on to his negative experiences rather than go against the family rules, and this particular session was no different to the previous ones. Margaret had unwittingly

assumed the role of Scott's unseeing and uninvolved mother, and Scott that of the compliant and affection-starved child. But beneath the mask of forced conformity to parental expectations, repressed rage and other shame-bound emotions throbbed; a storm was brewing. Something had abruptly awoken Scott's memories of feeling unwanted, unseen and unloved. He was sitting on his hands, staring at the floor, rocking back and forth.

Scott: *I don't know what's happening to me … this isn't right … I don't understand, I don't know what's happening.*

Margaret remained silent.

Scott: *I need to get out, I feel like I'm going to explode, do something!*

Margaret did not react. She remained still and calmly said: '*Stay with the feeling*'. Scott stood up, and within a split second, a lifetime of un-cried tears, hidden hurts and unfelt feelings exploded in a rage-fuelled outburst.

Scott: *Don't you fucking tell me to stay with it! I've been staying with that feeling for 20 years. I'm here 'cause I don't wanna stay with that feeling. I don't wanna stay with it anymore!*

Scott's sudden eruption might have been an unconscious attempt to rework the past, to force Margaret to go back with him to when his fearful child affects were not adequately regulated and to provide him with a healthier response than the one he was accustomed to. But she did not. Instead Margaret looked at Scott with her head slightly tilted to one side, one hand resting on the other, Mona Lisa style. Her face betrayed no emotions. She only replied with a low therapeutic '*um*'. And Scott sat down.

Scott: *Fine … Whatever … You know what, sometimes you're so fucking lifelike I forget you aren't human.*

Margaret's professional detachment had triggered a protective aggressive response, yet she was right. When she asked Scott to 'stay with it', she was merely encouraging him to experience the feeling fully and let it go all the way through him, like a lightning bolt through a lightning rod. For anything that moves does not hurt; it is only what stops in us that festers and infects our present with past hurts (Richo, 1997). When she invited Scott to stay with the feeling, she was echoing Wilson's words: 'stay in your bleakness; out of its blankness something will come' (2008, p34), for when we grant hospitality to our pains, we gain a fresh way of seeing, a new knowledge of our selves and the world. But Margaret's message did not come across that way. Scott did not hear: 'Stay with the unfamiliar presence and let's get to the core of it'. He heard: 'Suffer in silence, child'.

Margaret's lack of emotional engagement and affective holding confirmed Scott's beliefs that his experiences had no value. And once again, defeated by a world he perceived as hollow and uncaring, Scott returned to earlier patterns of behaviour. He banished his relational needs, shut down and remained silent for the rest of the session. The following week he decided to terminate treatment with Margaret and searched for a new therapist.

Joseph's approach was very different from that of Margaret; rather than be a 'blank canvas', Joseph fully engaged with his clients' experiences and often shared with them the emotional impact their affects had on him. Only two weeks after they first met, Scott had one of his episodes. Again, something had accidentally reawakened his childhood pain, and a terror was growing inside him. Scott was in panic mode, sweating, pulse racing, sitting on the edge of his chair, fingers tightly clenched around the armrests. He was rocking back and forth, staring at the ground and repeatedly telling he felt an explosion was about to happen, 'It's that thing again, I can't take it'. Joseph did not say a word, but his eyes replied. They were filled with tears. Rather than remain a distant observer, he joined Scott in his hurt and externalised what Scott had been defended against for so many years. Scott feared an explosion, but no explosion came. Joseph quietly cried Scott's un-cried tears

and Scott came out of hiding. He began to weep. Silent tears rolled down his cheeks, and he made no effort to stop them.

Through non-verbal channels of communication, Joseph gave a voice to Scott's quiet emotions. He conveyed the message that powerful feelings are part of what makes us human and tools that help us better understand our inner world. He showed Scott that authentic living requires not only the ability to expose our wounds to our fellow creatures but also the capacity to be affected by the wounds of others (Peck, 1988). And so Scott discovered that intense feelings could be deeply felt and survived. He acknowledged the pain he was never allowed to express and began to address the hurt of his childhood.

Mirroring

Non-verbal communication of thoughts, emotions and intentions long precede the evolution of verbal abilities (Darwin, 1872), and to this day it still remains our major form of exchange,[12] particularly in child and primary caregiver interactions. Infants rely on their immediate environment to help them modulate and make sense of their experiences. In early development, the face of the mother acts as a mirror in which the child gradually discovers his sense of self and increases both his social functioning and ability to regulate his own affects. This mirroring is essential for self-realisation and emotional growth (Winnicott, 1971). In other words, healthy emotional development depends on seeing one's self confirmed and valued by a sensitive and consistent other. As Schore confirms, '*visual stimulation, embedded in mutual gaze transactions between caregiver and infant, is an essential component of a growth promoting environment*' (1994, p91). (We will further explore this concept in chapter 14.)

On the contrary, when the caregiver fails to empathically mirror a particular range of emotion in her child, the child in turn will avoid expressing and

---

[12] Research shows that over 65 per cent of communication is non-verbal (Mehrabian, 1972).

feeling those same emotions, and as a result, '*entire ranges of emotion can begin to be obliterated from the repertoire for intimate relations*' (Goleman, 1996, p101). But emotional learning is lifelong and there is hope in reparative relationships. Goleman adds that social interactions continually reshape our working model of relationships and provide us with opportunities to correct biographical distortions, '*an imbalance at one point can be corrected later; it's an ongoing, lifelong process*' (1996, p101).

So, just like an attuned caregiver, Joseph, with tears in his eyes replied to Scott's unexpressed childhood hurt. And like a child who resolves and integrates painful emotional experiences through empathic mirroring, Scott acknowledged and explored his experiences as they took place in Joseph. He increased his capacity to be present with his feelings and resumed an emotional development that had become stalled. For feelings of fear, anger, pain or loss are the tunnel through which we must all pass to get to the other side: to self-awareness, understanding and wholeness (Rogers, 2001).

Conclusion

Like a lot of emotionally wounded children, Scott learned that showing vulnerability was tantamount to opening Pandora's box and to be taken over by all that he had learned to regard as shameful. But, to get to the core of any experience, one must feel the feelings associated with the experience or, in the words of the Bohemian-Austrian poet Rilke, '*the more still, more patient and more open we are when we are sad, so much the deeper and so much the more unswervingly does the new go into us, so much the better do we make it ours*' (1934, p35). However, when early survival depends upon hiding emotions or urges, uncovering what has been disowned, and not knowing what is going to emerge, can feel like a terrifying gamble.

Moments of stress and paralysis arise when we no longer hear our emotions living, and so the only thing which can help emotionally frozen adolescents return to creative living is our ability to feel for them what is intolerable or dangerous to themselves. To reawaken their attachment needs, a form of

re-parenting has to happen where the adult, like a good-enough mother, acts as an auxiliary ego in which the child can rediscover his inner truth, increase his social functioning and learn how to be both vulnerable and robust. But vulnerability, like trust, is a two-way street (Erskine *et al*, 1999). So to work with emotionally wounded young people implies that we need to be more than healers, teachers, providers or counsellors; we ought to be '*fellow travellers*' (Yalom, 2002). We must show them the way through personal modelling, and of course, we can only help them to go as far as we ourselves have gone or are willing to go (Anderson & Dartington, 1998). We too need to find an empathic witness who'll help us reconnect with all that could have brought us into conflicts with the people we depended upon in our early years.

Before we move on to the second part of this book and venture into the world of emotionally wounded adolescents, I think it is necessary to dedicate one last chapter to an important part of their environment: their parents. Next, we will explore why we need to join forces with them and how we can provide them with empathic support so that they do not pass on their legacy of pain to their children.

REFERENCES

Anderson R & Dartington A (1998) *Facing It Out: Clinical Perspectives on Adolescent Disturbance*, Karnac Books, London.

Darwin C (2009) *The Expression of the Emotions in Man and Animals*, Penguin Classics, London (first published in 1872).

Erskine R, Moursund J & Trautmann R (1999) *Beyond Empathy: A Therapy of Contact in Relationships*, Brunner-Routledge, London.

Goleman D (1996) *Emotional Intelligence: Why It Can Matter More than IQ*, Bloomsbury, London.

Mehrabian A (1972) *Silent Messages: Implicit Communication of Emotions and Attitudes*, Wadsworth Publishing, Belmont, CA.

49

Peck SM (1988) *The Different Drum: Community Making and Peace*, Touchstone, New York.

Richo D (1997) *When Love Meets Fear*, Paulist Press, Mahwah, NJ.

Rilke MR (2004) *Letters to a Young Poet*. Translated by Norton H. W. W. Norton, New York (first published in 1934).

Rogers N (2001) 'Person-Centered expressive arts: therapy, a path to wholeness', Rubin JA (ed), *Approaches to Art Therapy: Theory and technique*, 2nd edn, Brunner-Routledge, Philadelphia, PA.

Schore A (1994) *Affect Regulation ad the Origin of the Self: The Neurobiology of Emotional Development*, Lawrence Erlbaum Associates, Mahwah, NJ.

Shelley MW (1992) *Frankenstein or the Modern Prometheus*, Wordsworth Classics, Hertfordshire (first published in 1818).

Wilson E (2008) *Against Happiness*, Sarah Crichton Books, New York.

Winnicott DW (2006) *Playing and Reality*, Routledge Classics, London (first published in 1971).

Yalom I (2002) *The Gift of Therapy: Reflections on Being a Therapist*, Piatkus Books, London.

7

SYMPATHY FOR THE 'DEVIL'

The healthy man does not torture others,
generally it is the tortured who turn into torturers.

C. G. Jung

(*Psychological Reflections*, 1986, p221)

Zombies have invaded our TV and cinema screens. They have become one of the 21st century's most popular and ghastly monsters. As we sit in our darkened living rooms and passively watch legions of post-apocalyptic ghouls chasing an out-of-breath and terrified human down the street, we physically react. We gasp, our adrenaline goes up, our heart rate increases, our blood vessels dilate and our muscles tense. The plight of the hapless victim running for his dear life reverberates so loudly within us that our brain and body respond as if we were being chased. Our emotional response runs parallel to that of the character, and we feel empathic fear. Yet as soon as the innocent victim is bitten and transforms into one of the flesh-eating monsters, the second the prey turns into a hunter, our empathy dies along with his humanity. We impatiently wait for the human-turned-zombie to be put through a wood chipper or covered with gasoline and set on fire. As the opening epigraph attests, we quickly forget that the predator was once prey and that only the tortured torture (Jung, 1986). Similarly, we often fail to remember that abusers were often themselves victims of abuse long before their victims.

The man who was angry for 50 years

A couple of years ago I was asked to deliver a teacher training workshop on child sexual abuse prevention and intervention. I had based my talk on a case study, the story of Thomas, a young man who for the first three-and-a-half years of his life was used as a commodity to satisfy the sexual urges of his mother and her many boyfriends. A few minutes before the workshop began, the school principal warned me about one of her staff, George. She described him as an opinionated 50-year-old man with impressive anger management issues and labelled him a '*bully*' who was '*just as bad as the students*'. She then added that she'd stay in the room at all time to make sure I felt safe. Needless to say that after such warning I was rather anxious. However, during the six-hour-long workshop George did not say a word, nor did he take any notes. He did not interact with anybody, and nobody interacted with him. He only stared at me with a stern look as if he were silently questioning everything I said. At the end of the training, once most of the teachers had left the room, he approached me and introduced himself, '*My name is George. I have been angry for 50 years*'. He quietly revealed he had been physically abused by his alcoholic father and had always been too ashamed to talk about it. He also disclosed that he himself had been an abusive husband and father and as a result he had lost all contact with his wife and children. He then added: '*Now I understand why. I'm the same as Thomas. Where can I get some help?*'

The psycho-educational aspect of the training day allowed George to understand and acknowledge how his past trauma had impacted his ability to relate and why he had so often used others as an outlet for his childhood rage. The particular patterns of attachment behaviour shown by an individual reflect the experiences he has had with attachment figures earlier in his life (Bowlby, 1979). George was not mad, nor was he bad; he was a deeply wounded human being. His challenging behaviour and lack of emotional empathy were a natural response to the terror he experienced in his childhood. Or as Holocaust survivor Frankl puts it, '*an abnormal reaction to an abnormal situation is normal behaviour*' (1946, p32).

The habit of categorising mothers and fathers as good or bad is something most of us are guilty of. I cannot recount how often, when suffering from compassion fatigue or when caught up in my own self-righteousness, I condemned parents for the sins of their children. We find comfort in blame. I

Speechmark

certainly do. Yet being aware of their realities can bring compassion into our approach and help us muster the empathy necessary to help them support the young people in their care.

Princess Shrek

Sally was a young single mother in her late 20s whom I thought should have her parental rights terminated. During a parent-teacher meeting, she had unashamedly and openly confessed that despite her wish to be a good mother, she'd often overreact at the smallest annoyance and regularly hit Liam, her 11-year-old son. Her son's teacher suggested her that she meet me.

As Fitzgerald (1934) wrote, meeting Sally was like shaking hands with an empty glove, and the 'bad mother' label I had prematurely stamped her with fitted her as badly as the loud, heavy eye make-up she was wearing. She looked like a demure young actress auditioning for the role of a worn out call girl in a low-budget daytime drama. The instant I saw her I thought: '*this woman has an endless potential for being hurt*'. She smiled and stuck out her hand, '*I'm Liam's mum*'. I invited her into my office and after the usual social pleasantries, I asked her to tell me about herself.

Sally's voice was almost unintelligible; she spoke like a ventriloquist, hardly moving her lips. Listening to her was like watching a poorly dubbed foreign film in which the spoken words were out of sync with facial expressions. She did not mention her son but instead talked about her romantic life. After a long string of physically and emotionally abusive relationships, she had recently met a loving and passionate older man who cared deeply for her and Liam. But Sally did not feel the same; in fact she seemed terrified to be the object of such affectionate attention. Although she kept good eye contact, and appeared to be an open book willingly sharing intimate stories with whoever would listen, something did not sound right. While listening to her worries and heartaches I felt a sharp feeling of unease, a curious mixture of rage, despair and self-loathing. I could hardly focus on what she was saying.

Speechmark

Me: *Sally, I need to stop you. I am trying to understand what you are going through but something is getting in the way. I'm experiencing this deep and nagging feeling of inadequacy ... Does that make any sense to you?*

She looked perplexed.

Me: *How much do you like yourself?*

Sally: *Oh I hate myself!*

I was a little surprised by the manner in which she so casually replied.

Me: *What is it that you hate so much about yourself?*

Sally: *Everything.*

Me: *Everything is a lot.*

She responded with a protective smile. I smiled back.

Me: *You said you hate everything about yourself ... and that cannot be easy, yet you're wearing a big smile. I am feeling little a confused!*

She did not answer. She just smiled some more. That woman was already wearing me down and I felt the urge to slap the smile off her face. I inhaled a deep, long breath, paused, took stock of my feelings and silently wondered if she had unconsciously brought a piece of her own history into our relationship. Curious to explore her polarities, and hoping that play might offer an alternative form of communication, I invited her to select two objects from the large toy box, one to symbolise something she loathed about herself and another to represent something she liked. She agreed but requested that I looked away while she selected the toys. After a couple of minutes she asked me to turn around. She had placed a seashell on the table and said the second object was in her coat pocket.

Sally: *I couldn't think of anything I liked about myself,*
but when I saw that seashell it reminded me of my
childhood in Brighton.

Sally told me she spent three years living with her grandparents by the seaside and said she'd never forget how much fun they had together.

Me: *How old were you?*

Sally: *I went there when I was three. I stayed with them until I*
was six.

Me: *What about your parents?*

Sally: *They were in London … I stopped talking when I was*
three years old, they didn't know what to do with me …
I think that's why they sent me to my grandparents.

Me: *You stopped talking when you were three! In my*
experience little girls love to talk. I'm wondering if you
were a happy child.

Sally: *Uh … I dunno … I never thought about it that way.*

Her voice was almost childlike.

Me: *What was it like when you returned to your parents' home?*

Sally: *They argued a lot … Dad pushed Mum down the stairs.*

Me: *That would have been very scary for a little girl to see*
her dad push her mum down the stairs.

Sally: *I guess.*

Her face betrayed no emotions. As we were nearing the end of our session, I wondered about the toy hidden in her coat pocket, but Sally refused to take it out.

Me:	*How about we play a little game? You give me a clue and I try to guess what's hiding inside your pocket.*

She agreed.

Sally:	*I am green.*
Me:	*Are you a vegetable?*
Sally:	*No.*
Me:	*Could I have another clue?*
Sally:	*I am green and I am fat.*
Me:	*Are you a fat caterpillar?*

She shook her head.

Me:	*I'm really stuck … I think I need one more clue.*
Sally:	*I'm green and I'm fat and I'm disgusting.*

Before I had time to venture another guess, Sally reached for her coat pocket and pulled out an action figure, Fiona from the animated movie *Shrek*, in which a princess is cursed to transform into a hideous green ogress at sunset. On the back of the toy she had written the word 'ugly' with a permanent marker.

Sally:	*I'm fat, I'm ugly, I'm disgusting. I'm Fiona from* Shrek.
Me:	*If you think you are so fat and so ugly and so disgusting, I understand why you want to stay hidden.*
Sally:	*I was raped you know!*

It felt like someone had suddenly emptied a bucket of iced water on my head.

Speechmark

Me: *When were you raped?*

Sally: *Twelve years ago.*

Sally's son was 11! She disclosed that her next-door neighbour assaulted her at the age of 16 and that after her parents found out, they reinforced her abuser's wishes and forbade her to tell anybody about it. Nine months later Liam was born, her neighbour moved out, and Sally's abuse remained a well-kept secret. When recounting her traumatic memories Sally remained calm and collected. She appeared indifferent to her own injuries.

Me: *Sally, you were a child; it must have been terrifying. And you had no one you could talk to ... It's awfully brave of you to share your pain with me.*

I felt a lump form in my throat and tears well up in my eyes, and I did not fight them back; she needed to see the impact her story had on me.

Me: *Do you think that when you look at Liam, it brings back all the hurts and all the pains you were not allowed to talk about?*

Timid tears formed in her eyes, and she sobbed quietly.

Sally: *I never thought about it that way.*

Reflection

It is common for abuse survivors to wall off emotional memories associated with past trauma and to unconsciously recreate in the here-and-now the very tragedy they seek to be put right (Zulueta, 1993). When I further explored the powerful emotions Sally had aroused in me, how I first perceived her as a vacuous woman with loose morals, how frustrated I felt and how tempted I was to violently wipe the smile off her face, I realised that my responses not only were similar to how her neighbour had treated her but also mirrored dynamics played out in her family environment as well as her interactions with her son. British psychoanalyst Joan Raphael-Leff remarks that in the eyes of the mother, a child conceived in violence remains '*part stranger, likely to be ostracized or punished*' (1990, p129). For 12 years Sally had tried to forget and remove herself from the pains of her childhood, but when her son behaved in an unexpected manner that most would shake off with a shrug, Sally's past intruded in the present and impinged on her ability to be the mother she wished to be. '*Dissociation is almost always a concomitant of sexual abuse in childhood*', remarks Elizabeth Howell (2005, p108). In echoing the works of Davies and Frawley (1994), she notes that adult survivors of childhood abuse have to split their experience of self into two parts: the external 'business as usual' part that manages to keep things together and the unseen child part that nobody talks about. This was the part that Sally's son often unwittingly triggered. In philosopher and rape survivor Susan Brison's words, '*trauma not only haunts the conscious and unconscious mind, but also remains in the body, in each of the senses, ready to resurface whenever something triggers a reliving of the traumatic event*' (2002, x). The survivor must find an empathic listener, for even though simply sharing the traumatic past is in itself insufficient for psychological healing, '*saying something about the memory does something to it*' (xi).

A few days after Sally and I first met, her son's teacher reported that during circle time, Liam revealed that he and his mother had spent the evening cuddling each other while watching television. It was the first time he had experienced that closeness. Sally and I carried on working together for a few months. She also agreed to attend a basic parenting course. Over time, not only did her relationship with her son gradually strengthen, but she also managed to develop some empathy for her own wounded inner child.

Conclusion

Challenging adolescents are not born of evil parentage. The majority of parents want the very best for their children, but those who did not

experience loving infant-caregiver attachment patterns and whose early development was contaminated by fear, deprivation or coercive control, cannot give what they never received. Just as secure attachment patterns repeat across generations, so too do dysfunctional ones (Blaustein & Kinniburgh, 2010). As Richo puts it, 'we mostly relate in the present with one foot in the past' (2008, p165). The adults we label unfit for parenthood are not heartless monsters, immoral perverts or sadistic freaks. They are survivors of adverse childhood experiences who are still haunted by the terrors of bygone years. Like Sally and George, they are wounded souls whose present is not different from their past – only subtly disguised – a past that also bears striking similarities to that of the young people we work with. To label them achieves nothing, for blame is just a naive way of making sense of the chaos (Coupland, 2001), and chaos is nothing but patterns we have not yet identified. Unless we become aware of such patterns and provide empathic support to emotionally wounded mothers and fathers, they'll pass on their legacy of pain to their own children, and history will repeat itself.

In the first part of *I, Monster* we have explored how relational failures echo across generations, how authentic living depends upon our capacity to reconnect empathically with the estranged and unloved parts of our selves and how we first need to acknowledge our unmet needs before we can empathise with those of others. We are now going to turn our attention to the inner world of troubled and troubling adolescents, the so-called 'feral teens'.

REFERENCES

Blaustein M & Kinniburgh K (2010) *Treating Traumatic Stress in Children and Adolescents: How to Foster Resilience through Attachment, Self-regulation, and Competency*, Guilford Press, New York.

Bowlby J (2005) *The Making And Breaking of Affectional Bonds*, Routledge Classics, Oxon (first published in 1979).

Speechmark

Brison S (2002) *Aftermath: Violence and the Remaking of a Self*, Princeton University Press, Princeton, NJ.

Coupland D (2001) *All Families Are Psychotic*, Flamingo, London.

Davies J & Frawley M (1994) *Treating the Adult Survivor of Childhood Sexual Abuse*, Basic Books, New York.

Fitzgerald FS (2012) *Tender is the Night*, William Collins, UK (first published in 1934).

Frankl V (2004) *Man's Search for Meaning*, Rider, London (first published in 1946).

Howell E (2005) *The Dissociative Mind*, Routledge, New York.

Jung C (1986) *Psychological Reflections: A New Anthology of His Writings 1905–1961*, Routledge, East Sussex.

Raphael-Leff J (1990) 'Psychotherapy and pregnancy', published in Journal of Reproductive and Infant Psychology, Vol. 8, No. 2. London: Routledge; April 1990.

Richo D (2008) *When the Past is Present: Healing the Emotional Wounds that Sabotage Our Relationships*, Shambala, Boston, MA.

Zulueta de F (1993) *From Pain to Violence: The Traumatic Roots of Destructiveness*, Whurr Publishing, London.

PART 2

The inner world of the troubled teen

8

TAMING THE WILD THINGS

I remember my own childhood vividly. I knew terrible things.
But I knew I mustn't let adults know I knew. It would scare them.

Maurice Sendak

(*The New Yorker*, 27 September 1993)

When it was first published in the fall of 1963, *Where the Wild Things Are* was the subject of vehement attacks and criticisms from school librarians, professors and psychologists who accused Sendak of having written a disturbing book containing images and text unsuitable for young children. One critic cautioned, '*it is not a book to be left where a sensitive child may come upon it at twilight*' (Lanes, 2013, p104). Since then it has gone on to sell millions of copies all around the world, has inspired numerous children stories on the theme 'taming the wilderness within' and is now widely recognised as one of the classics of modern children's literature (Lassen-Seger, 2006).

The wilds of the psyche

Sendak's celebrated masterpiece recounts the adventures of Max, a securely attached and mischievous six-year-old boy with a healthy play drive. The book opens with our small hero dressed in wolf pyjamas making '*mischief of one kind and another*'. We see him hammering large nails into his bedroom walls, running down the stairs and terrorizing his dog with a fork, until his exhausted mother calls him a '*Wild Thing*' and sends him to bed without any supper.[13]

---

[13] In the second frame, as Max is chasing the family pet down the stairs, we can see a child drawing tacked to the wall. It depicts one of the monsters we are about to meet and is signed 'by Max'. This suggests that the Island of the Wild Things is a place that Max has already visited. As Sendak notes, '*Max [...] believes in a flexible world of fantasy and reality, a world where a child can skip from one to the other and back again in the sure belief that both really exist*' (1989, p152).

Max's boisterous and out-of-bounds behaviour is typical of his age. Like most six-year-olds, he is growing more daring and more adventurous. His drive towards independence is gathering momentum, but this wish for autonomous living causes him much anxiety. On the one hand he wants to separate from the adults around him and wants the freedom to do as he pleases, but on the other hand he is not yet ready to let go of his mother's love and support. He wants both and finds it almost impossible to choose (Bates Ames & Frances, 1979). As Cech notes, '*it is a basic problem for a child to express those volatile emotions that are part of an emerging self when to do so threatens to fracture the very bonds of love that he wishes to preserve and upon which he relies*' (1995, p120).[14]

To deal with these ungovernable and dangerous forces, Max turns to fantasy. In the next frame, alone in his bedroom with nothing to eat, he closes his eyes and escapes into the wilderness of his own psyche. The bedposts transform into trees, the rug turns into a grassy path and a magical forest begins to grow '*until the walls [become] the world all around*'. Our young traveller finds himself on an imaginary boat sailing towards a far-off land inhabited by five fierce creatures of fur and teeth. When he arrives to the place where the Wild Things are, '*they [roar] their terrible roars, and [gnash] their terrible teeth*', but Max tames them all '*with the magic trick of staring into all their yellow eyes, without blinking once*', a trick that only securely attached children who have received responsive and consistent caregiving can perform (Kagan, 2009). Max is immediately hailed as their king. However, after befriending the powerful emotions that rage within him and much '*wild rumpus*', Max grows homesick. He longs to be '*where someone [loves] him best of all*'. So, he gives up his crown, steps into his imaginary boat and leaves the Wild Things behind. He sails back to reality and returns to his

---

[14] Louise Bates Ames (1979), the American Psychologist and co-founder of the Gesell Institute of Child Development, states that the typical six-year-old loves to dress up and engage in pretend games. He is almost constantly active, often rough in play and enthusiastic for new ideas and new adventures. He is also a paradoxical little person; he wants to be close to his mother and at the same time wants his independence.

Speechmark

mother's love, his secure base (Bowlby, 1988).[15] In the last frame, a smiling Max in his bedroom pushes back the hood of the wolf suit, becomes a little boy again and finds his dinner still warm and waiting for him. He has returned from his dream journey more self-aware and better equipped to regulate his emotions. Not only has he learned to master the destructive forces that threatened to rupture the emotional bond between him and his mother, but he has discovered that even when he behaves like a little monster, he will still be loved.[16] Dr Willet, a researcher at the Centre for the Study of Children, Youth and Media, remarks: '*This is a classic hero's story [...] the protagonist undertakes a journey and returns a wiser person*' (*The Guardian*, 2009).

Less than a year after its publication, *Where the Wild Things Are* won the Caldecott Award for the best picture book of the year. During his acceptance speech, Sendak explained: '*From their earliest years, children live on familiar terms with disrupting emotions [...] and it is through fantasy that children achieve catharsis. It is the best means they have for taming wild things*' (1989, p151). Thus for securely attached children who have learned to trust their environment and use their mother as a secure base from which to explore, fantasy is not just an attempt to escape from reality: it is a way of making sense of it. It allows them to connect the inner world of the psyche to the outer world of reality (Person, 1995). It is through imaginative and make-believe play that they learn about themselves, discover the world around them and develop their capacity to respond creatively and flexibly to life situations. Flights of imagination allow them to safely address and discharge real fears and anxieties as well as explore new possibilities and try on new behaviour without being directly at risk (Brown, 2009).

---

[15] John Bowlby notes that a sensitive, responsive, caring and consistent caregiver acts as a 'secure base' from which the child can explore his surroundings and to which he can return when distressed. He defines a secure base as '*the provision by both parents of a secure base from which a child or adolescent can make sorties into the outside world and to which he can return knowing for sure that he will be welcomed when he gets there, nourished physically and emotionally, comforted if distressed, reassured if frightened*' (1988, p12).

[16] An animated version of Maurice Sendak's story book can be watched on www.youtube.com/watch?v=aw0_f9xLHfo

---

Conclusion

A large body of research highlights the link between pretend play and impulse control. Person (1995) notes that these games counter feelings of powerlessness. They allow the child to regulate emotional turmoil and permit him to replace passivity with activity and helplessness with mastery. Singer (1973) observes that the more children engage in fantasy play, the more controlled their overt behaviour and the more empathetic they are towards the suffering of others. Conversely, children who lack opportunities to play show high egocentricity, poor self-soothing abilities and low interpersonal skills (Fisher & Fisher, 1993). May (1998) adds that those who have not had the freedom to explore and work out their destructive urges in fantasy act them out in reality. This idea was confirmed by clinical researchers who worked with violent young men in prisons and found that play deprivation in childhood is a key predictor of criminality (Brown, 2009). Although make-believe games facilitate emotional growth, promote socialisation and even sharpen the skills needed to make fine reality-unreality distinctions (Fisher & Fisher, 1993), playing with unreality has a darker side: it can isolate the 'dreamer' from real human relationships.

Nearly 50 years after Max was first crowned 'king of all the Wild Things', Maurice Sendak's beloved monsters leaped from the pages of the picture book onto the cinema screen. In Spike Jonze's (2009) cinematic version, as Max leaves his wild life and title behind him, one of the monsters says softly, '*You are the first king we haven't eaten*'. Unfortunately, as we will find out in the next chapter, not all children who escape into the wilds of their psyche are that lucky, some end up consumed by fear and feelings of worthlessness. For only the resilient and the securely attached can tame their wild things and find their way back home. The oppressed and the emotionally deprived get eaten. In the absence of a safe secure base to return to, they surrender their self to a powerful bestial substitute and let their fictions dominate their lives.

REFERENCES

Bates Ames L & Frances L (1979) *Your Six-Year-Old: Loving and Defiant*, Dell Publishing, New York.

Bowlby J (2005) *A Secure Base*, Routledge, Oxon (first published in 1988).

Brown S (2009) *Play: How It Shapes the Brain, Opens the Imagination, and Invigorates the Soul*, Avery, New York.

Cech J (1995) *Angels and Wild Things: The Archetypal Poetics of Maurice Sendak*, Pennsylvania State University Press, University Park, PA.

Fisher S & Fisher R (1993) *The Psychology of Adaptation to Absurdity: Tactics of Make-believe*, Psychology Press, New York.

Jonze S (2009) *Where the Wild Things Are*, Warner Bros, Burbank, CA.

Kagan R (2009) 'Transforming troubled children into tomorrow's heroes', Brom D, Pat-Horenczyk R & Julian Ford D (eds), *Treating Traumatized Children: Risk, Resilience and Recovery*, Routledge, East Sussex.

Lanes S (2013) *The Art of Maurice Sendak*, Abrams, New York.

Lassen-Seger M (2006) *Adventures into Otherness*, Abo Akademi University Press, Finland.

May R (1998) *Power and Innocence: A Search for the Sources of Violence*, W. W. Norton, New York.

Person E (1995) *By Force of Fantasy: How We Make Our Lives*, Basic Books, New York.

Sendak M (1963) *Where the Wild Things Are*, Harper and Row, New York.

Sendak M (1989) *Caldecott & Co. Notes on Books and Pictures*, Reinhardt Books, London.

Sendak M (1993) 'In the dumps: conversation with Art Spiegelman', *The New Yorker*, 27th September 1993.

Singer J (1973) *The Child's World of Make Believe: Experimental Studies of Imaginative Play*, Academic Press, New York.

Thorpe V & Asthana A (2009) 'New film Where the Wild Things Are sends parents into a rumpus', published in *The Guardian*, 18th October 2009.

9

DEVOURED

*If you fail him, it must feel to him
as if the wild beasts will gobble him up.*

D. W. Winnicott

(*The Child And The Family*, 1957, p11)

In his acceptance speech for the Caldecott Award, Maurice Sendak read a letter he received from a seven-year-old fan: '*How much does it cost to get to where the wild things are? If it is not too expensive my sister and I want to spend the summer there. Please answer soon*'. Sendak did not reply; he knew that sooner or later, they would find their own way '*free of charge*' (Sendak, 1989). I am sure they did, yet I wonder if like Max, they managed to tame their wild things and find their way back to reality, as not all children who escape into the wilds of their psyche return. David McKee's classic picture book *Not Now, Bernard* (1980)[17] tells the story of such a boy who, in the absence of a safe and secure base to return to, becomes the victim of his fictions and makes a beast of himself.

Not now, Bernard

Bernard is a child brought up in an environment that is relentlessly cold and unresponsive. He is a little younger than Max; he looks about five. Unlike Sendak's six-year-old hero whose drive for independence and exploration makes life difficult for those around, the typical five-year-old would rather stay in the house than go out to play. Bates Ames notes that his mother is the centre of his world and he wants to be near her: '*[He] wants to talk with her, play with her, help her with her housework, follow her around the house*' (1979, p3). She adds that the five-year-old lives mostly in the here-and-now: '*The time that interests him is now, the place he likes best, here*' (p4). But

---

17 An animated version of *Not Now, Bernard* can be watched on www.youtube.com/watch?v=6ptST-5w6tU

for Bernard, the 'now' never comes. His parents are too busy to notice him and persistently dismiss his countless pleas for love with a sharp '*Not now, Bernard*'.

The book opens with Bernard desperately trying to attract his parents' attention, but Dad is doing DIY and Mum is busy in the kitchen. Every time he tries to speak to them they answer with the same refrain '*Not Now, Bernard*'.

In every frame their facial expressions and gestures convey indifference. Their backs are turned and their eyes are closed or focused elsewhere. They do not see their son. In a desperate attempt to be noticed, Bernard warns his mother of a terrifying monster lurking in their backyard, but his warning is unheeded. So, hands in his pockets, Bernard goes outside, down the steps and into the garden where a purple-blue creature with little horns and jagged teeth waits for him. Undaunted by meeting the terrible beast, Bernard looks straight into its eyes and tries to befriend it. But only securely attached children can tame their wild things with the magic trick of staring unblinkingly into their eyes, and unlike Sendak's young hero, Bernard does not have a warm and responsive relationship with his caregivers. In the next frame the monster eats him up, '*every bit*'. The child who longed for love and validation is no more. Bernard is now inside the creature. He has become the victim of his fiction. He has become the monster.[18] The way he perceives the world also changes. His house turns red, the sky purple and the trees now bear a striking resemblance to those found on Max's island. His world has now become a more threatening and dangerous place.

But the child-turned-monster still longs for validation. He re-enters the house and tries to attract his parents' attention. He roars at his mum and bites his

---

[18] McDougall's theatrical production of McKee's classic (2014) confirms that the monster eating up Bernard is a symbolic metamorphosis. After facing the creature, the actor playing Bernard (Rhys Rusbatch) dons the monster costume. He transforms into the beast. Fisher and Fisher (1993) notes that five-year-olds can get so caught up in pretend play that they momentarily become hazy about the distinction between what is real and what is not, and, like Bernard, they can be subsumed by their fantasies.

---

father's leg, but the same monotonous refrain continues '*Not Now, Bernard*'. Every time he is rebuffed, he looks straight at the reader with wide-opened eyes and a puzzled look, as if he were trying to engage us and as if he were thinking: '*I don't understand what's happening here. What have I done wrong?*' In the next page, his mother calls, '*Your dinner is ready*'. She puts a plate of sausages, chips and peas in front of the television and leaves the room before her son enters. But this is not the kind of nourishment Bernard craves. He wants love. He wants warmth and affection.[19] Driven by his own instincts he tips the plate in his mouth, makes a mess, jumps on the telly and climbs all over the furniture. To discharge his rage against his unfeeling mother, he violently throws a toy robot against a wall, for this is how children communicate their hurt; they use toys as their words and re-enact in their play what has been done to them (Landreth, 2001). But his busy mother still fails to notice him. Her eyes are closed. She calls: '*Go to bed, I've taken up your milk*'. Bernard walks upstairs, dragging a teddy bear behind him. His failure to elicit a response from his caregivers shows in his posture. His head is down, his shoulders hunched and his body slack. In the last double-page spread, the child-turned-monster is tucked in bed with his teddy bear. '*But I am a monster*', he softly whimpers. His mother looks away. She turns off the light and replies, '*Not now, Bernard*'.

Bernard's story is a tragic contemporary tale in which nobody lives happily ever after. It does not follow the traditional circular narrative of most children book (Waller, 2009). At the end, Bernard still remains unseen and bound to his bestial form; his metamorphosis from a needy and love-seeking little boy into a savage beast goes unacknowledged and unresolved.

David McKee's seemingly simple narrative not only confirms that children need to be seen, it also provides us with an understanding of the survival kit of emotionally wounded adolescents.

---

[19] Echoing the work of Lendon Smith (1976), Bates Ames and Frances (1979) remarks that if the frontal cortex (the impulse-control part of the brain) is not properly nourished and nurtured with love from a responsive caregiver, the animal brain takes over and the child becomes aggressive.

Speechmark ⑤

The importance of being seen

Lassen-Seger (2006) notes that although the issue of being seen is not directly mentioned in McKee's text, it lies at the heart of every picture. Page after page the visual narrative suggests that self-realisation and emotional well-being depend upon the confirmation of one's self as unique by a sensitive and consistent other. Bernard's ordeal parallels in many ways the 'Still Face' experiment (Tronick, 2007) in which a mother is asked to stop interacting with her infant and assume a non-responsive stance. Immediately the child picks up on the change and desperately attempts to get his mother to re-engage. He smiles, grimaces, points, protests and screams. Eventually, he loses postural control and collapses. He disengages and retreats into himself. In other words, this failure of external mirroring is re-enacted internally as a repudiation of the needy and love-seeking aspects of the self (Mollon, 2001). Goleman remarks, *'when such encounters become typical of child and parent, they mold the child's emotional expectations about relationships, outlooks that will flavor [his] functioning in all realms of life'* (1996, p193). He adds that neglect can have more damaging consequences than outright abuse.

As they grow up, children experience new feelings and emotions; however, their repertoire of coping strategies is far more limited than ours. They rely on their immediate environment to contain their powerful emotions and help them make sense of their experiences. Becoming aware of negative and aggressive feelings can be very frightening for them. Brazelton (2002) argues that the mean monsters that invade their fantasies sometimes represent the strain of facing these 'new' feelings. In order to manage such disruptive emotions and increase their abilities to regulate their own affects, they need to have them contained and then reflected back by an empathic caregiver. As we will further explore in chapter 14, the role of the mother as a container for the child's anxieties is key to healthy emotional development. Conversely, as *Not Now, Bernard* illustrates, the prolonged lack of maternal responsiveness renders the child invisible and may contribute to the development of a fantastic omnipotent self to help him survive in a world in which he feels helpless and worthless.

The fantastic omnipotent self

McKee's dramatic narrative attests to how a child deprived of affirmation and empathic attunement experiences acute helplessness. Unable to find comfort, warmth or protection in the outside world, his only option is to withdraw from his environment and take refuge in fantasy. He lays aside his need to love and be loved and unconsciously creates a mighty inner rescuer, a fantastic and omnipotent self that hides any trace of vulnerability and protects from humiliation and abandonment (Taransaud, 2011). His fate echoes Johnson's famous quote, '*He who makes a beast of himself gets rid of the pain of being a man*' (2007, p333); after all, it is better to be a monster than to be nothing. Yet any sense of security gained only offers temporary respite, for the defences he relies upon denies him the very thing he seeks. What first appears to offer an instant solution to life's problems keeps him tied to an anti-developmental alliance with an oppressive omnipotent self that inhibits both the expression and awareness of needs. In other words, it keeps the vulnerable and needy parts of the self cut off from emotional intimacy (Taransaud, 2011).

McKee's picture book offers a window into the inner world of the troubled and troubling teen. Like Bernard, although his behaviour may at times appear monstrous, far beneath the aggressive facade, the exiled love-seeking part of the self is still alive, yearning for what it has been deprived of, tenderness and environmental stability. Like McKee's child-turned-monster, the so-called 'feral youth' is still longing to rediscover his lost humanity in the loving gaze of a responsive other. His antisocial behaviour is nothing more than a desperate attempt to coerce his environment to provide him with the validation and the maternal care he never received (Winnicott, 1967).

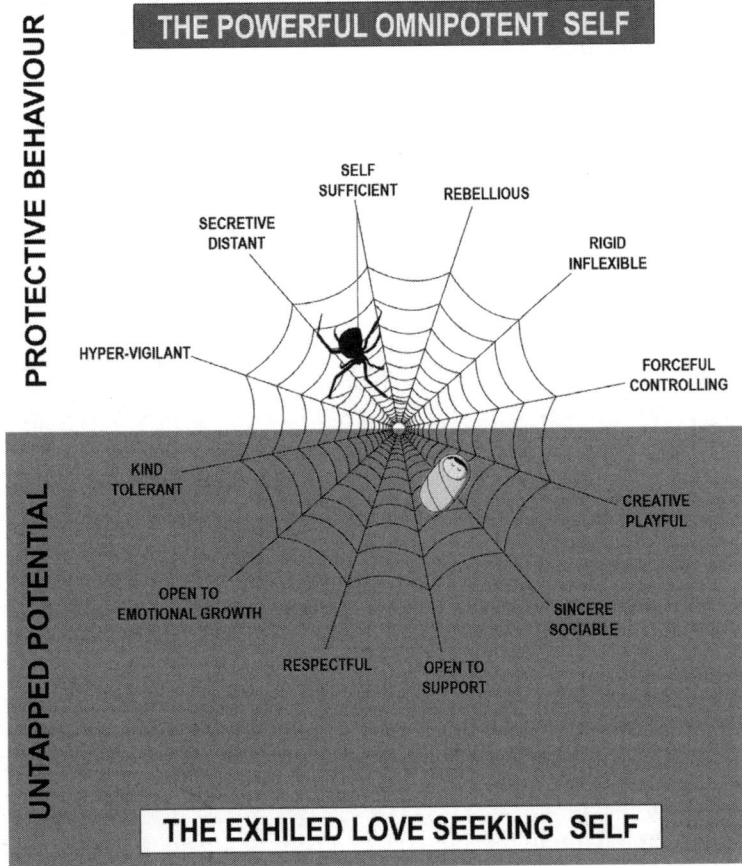

PROTECTIVE BEHAVIOUR

THE POWERFUL OMNIPOTENT SELF

SELF SUFFICIENT

REBELLIOUS

SECRETIVE DISTANT

RIGID INFLEXIBLE

HYPER-VIGILANT

FORCEFUL CONTROLLING

KIND TOLERANT

CREATIVE PLAYFUL

UNTAPPED POTENTIAL

OPEN TO EMOTIONAL GROWTH

SINCERE SOCIABLE

RESPECTFUL

OPEN TO SUPPORT

THE EXHILED LOVE SEEKING SELF

Conclusion

When faced with difficulties, securely attached children have the ability to cross the boundary between the real and the imaginary. Their play and brief sojourn into fantasy allows them to make sense of the world, promotes their social and emotional development and enhances their creative thinking and problem-solving skills. In short, momentary escapes into fantasy can strengthen their reality functioning. But for the child who has been repeatedly deprived of maternal love, fantasy can act as a poor substitute for an unsatisfactory reality. It takes over the growing self, overrides the child's natural desire to bond with others with fear and control, dominates his inner life and eventually becomes integral to his sense of self. In other words, trapped in his fantasy and with no conceivable way out, the child not only becomes the victim of his fictions, he may also act them out. And this can have dire consequences.

On 20 April 1999, at precisely 23:19, Eric Harris and Dylan Klebold, two high school seniors, pulled an arsenal of shotguns, semiautomatic machine pistols and small homemade bombs from beneath their trench coats. They opened fire on their classmates and teachers, massacred 13 people and wounded 23 before turning their weapons on themselves. In a video the boys made the night before the shooting, Harris mimicked his parents saying: '*If only we had checked his room. If only we had asked more questions*'. In his book *Killing Monsters: Why Children Need Fantasy, Superheroes and Make-Believe Violence*, Jones (2002) mentions the findings of James McGee, an expert on juvenile forensic psychology. After he studied all the threats and destructive fantasies chronicled for 18 months on Harris's website and in the boys' journals, McGee discovered that one thread ran through nearly every minute and page: the wish to be seen, to be noticed. I am not suggesting that young people who experience neglect will engage in such extreme destructive acts; I simply wish to illustrate how in the absence of validation, affirmation and empathy, children learn to rely on a poor substitute, the illusion of power. As Dylan Klebold wrote in his diary: '*The lonely man strikes with absolute rage*' (Marsico, 2011).

But fortunately hope remains, '*fantasy narratives are continually modified by new input from the external world […] there is always potential for reconfiguring one's fantasy life and one's psyche*' (Person, 1995, p70). In chapters 14–21, we will discuss how emotionally nourishing interactions, together with a willingness to enter the perceptual world of wounded teens, can heal the pain of the past and help the frightened captive self find its way back home. However, before we explore how to help adolescents return to creative living, let us venture deeper into their inner landscapes and explore what might happen to McKee's disconsolate young hero as he grows older. In the next chapter we will meet with a real-life Bernard: Dennis Avner, or, as he preferred to be called, 'Stalking Cat'.

REFERENCES

Bates Ames L & Frances L (1979) *Your Five-Year-Old: Sunny and Serene*, Dell Publishing, New York.

Brazelton TB (2002) *Touchpoints: Three to Six*, Da Capo Press, Boston, MA.

Fisher S & Fisher R (1993) *The Psychology of Adaptation to Absurdity: Tactics of Make-believe*, Psychology Press, New York.

Goleman D (1996) *Emotional Intelligence: Why It Can Matter More than IQ*, Bloomsbury, London.

Johnson S (2007) *Johnsonian Miscellanies*, Vol. 2 – Arranged and edited by Birkbeck G. Oxford University Press, Oxford.

Jones G (2002) *Killing Monsters: Why Children Need Fantasy, Superheroes and Make-believe Violence*, Basic Books, New York.

Landreth G (2001) *Innovations in Play Therapy: Issues, Process, and Special Populations*, Routledge, New York.

Lassen-Seger M (2006) *Adventures into Otherness*, Abo Akademi University Press, Finland.

Marsico K (2011) *The Columbine High School Massacre: Murder in the Classroom*, Marshall Cavendish, New York.

McDougall E (2014) *Not Now Bernard (Theatre Play)*, The Unicorn Theatre, London.

McKee D (1980) *Not Now, Bernard*, Andersen Press, London.

Mollon P (2001) *Releasing the Self: The Healing Legacy of Heinz Kohut*, Whurr, London.

Person E (1995) *By Force of Fantasy: How We Make Our Lives*, Basic Books, New York.

Sendak M (1989) *Caldecott & Co. Notes on Books and Pictures*, Reinhardt Books, London.

Smith L (1976) *Improving Your Child's Behaviour Chemistry*, Prentice Hall, Upper Saddle River, NJ.

Taransaud D (2011) *You Think I'm Evil: Practical Strategies for Working with Aggressive and Challenging Adolescents*, Worth Publishing, London.

Tronick E (2007) *The Neurobehavioral and Social-Emotional Development of Infants and Children*, Norton, NewYork.

Waller A (2009) *Constructing Adolescence in Fantastic Realism*, Routledge, New York.

Winnicott D (1986) Delinquency as a Sign of Hope; a talk given to the Borstal Assistant Governors' Conference, held at King Alfred's College, Winchester, April 1967, published in Home is Where we Start From. London: Penguin Books; 1990 (first published in 1967).

Winnicott D (2011) *The Child and the Family, First relationships*. Routledge, Oxon (first published in 1957).

10

THE CALL OF THE WILD

You made us in the house of pain!
You made us … things! Not men! Not beasts!
Part man … part beast! Things!

Sayer of the Law – played by Bela Lugosi
(E. Kenton. *Island of Lost Souls*, Paramount Pictures, 1932)

Escapes into fantasy and the adoption of an animal identity (either the individual turns into one, behaves like one or dresses up like one) is a characteristic theme of many folk tales and well-known children books. When we deconstruct some of these narratives, such as *Where The Wild Things Are* and *Not Now, Bernard*, we discover that depending on the relational environment in which the child grows up, the significance of child-animal metamorphosis stories varies: either the transformation is fluid and implies a rebirth, or the transformation is irreversible and suggests an entrapment of self. When the child comes from a secure, loving background, the transformation is a temporary retreat, where he eventually returns to his human self enriched with a deeper level of awareness, a more flexible approach to life and a far richer connection with himself and his environment. In short, he learns to tame his wild things and discovers that despite adversity, a full and creative life is within his reach (Bettelheim, 1976). On the contrary, stories of irreversible child-animal metamorphoses do not suggest personal growth but an engulfment of the soul and loss of emotional intimacy and creative freedom; they are linked to issues of abandonment and terrifying helplessness. The child deprived of warmth, safety and appropriate maternal care surrenders his autonomy and allows a powerful bestial substitute to dominate his psychic life while his vulnerable human self, subdued and flattened, is condemned to dwell in an emotional wasteland (Taransaud, 2011). And as this chapter highlights, without the opportunity to merge with the goodness of a caring other, these fantasies persist throughout a lifetime and ultimately annihilate the entire self.

Speechmark Ⓢ

Stalking cat: the manimal

On his journey towards adulthood, the Native American Indian youth must go on a Vision Quest and find his guiding spirit through fasting and isolated meditation in the deep wilderness. He is warned that on his dream journey he will be accosted by the spirit of the Windigo, a lonesome and depraved anthropophagous monster with a heart of ice and an insatiable appetite for human flesh. The novice is instructed that unless he rejects the evil spirit forcefully, he will sink into melancholic withdrawal, succumb to an irreversible bestial metamorphosis, and *'turn Windigo'* (Gilmore, 2003).[20] Dennis was one of these individuals who had traumatically bonded with a ferocious predator and turned feral in appearance.

In February 2008, Dennis Avner, a descendant of the Huron tribe of Native American Indians, earned a world record for permanent body modifications. For over 30 years Dennis, often better known as Stalking Cat (his Native American Indian name), surgically altered his body to resemble that of his totem animal, the tiger. Dennis's extreme cosmetic procedures, which were performed without any anaesthetic, included bifurcation of his upper lip, ear elongation, transdermal implants in his forehead and cheeks, tiger stripe tattoos and facial piercings on either side of his restructured nose through which he could insert synthetic whiskers. He also wore fanged dentures, an animatronic tiger tail and contact lenses with slit irises. The painful surgeries he underwent turned him into a media sideshow curiosity, a *deviant* lost somewhere between man and beast.

Dennis was fond of saying, he *'found fame, but never fortune'* (Larratt, 2012). He spent the last six years of his life in a trailer at the back of a hardware store in Tonopah, Nevada, with three cats he called his children. In interviews, when asked about his social life, Dennis answered that he

---

[20] The Windigo confrontation parallels one of the central tasks of adolescence individuation, the need to confront the more destructive aspects of the self, the Shadow. As Guggenbuhl-Craig remarks, *'Young people must have contact with the Devil, but they must on no account identify with him'* (1971, p118). We will explore this concept further in the following chapter.

---

preferred the company of felines to that of humans and that being a tiger was more important to him than humanity (*Daily Mail*, 2008). Although Dennis claimed that his transformation was out of respect for an ancient Huron tradition, in his last televised interviews, for the first time, he allowed the world to see beneath the cat persona. Dennis revealed a childhood devastated by loss, abandonment and abuse. He disclosed he never really knew his father and that his stepfather was a *'child molester'*. When asked if he had been a victim, Dennis calmly replied, *'Not to a great extent, but enough. I mean, I've got some mental trauma that'll never go away'* (Channel 4, 2010).

Shattered sense of safety

Having been abused by an early attachment figure, Dennis was forced to experience closeness and betrayal at the same time and internalised the link between them. The abuse-related internalisation *'I am betrayed by people close to me'* (Wieland, 1998) had not only altered his inner model of self but also shattered his sense of safety. He lived in a state of constant hypervigilance, stuck in survival mode, always scanning for threats in his immediate environment (Potts, 2007). In the 2002 documentary *Animal Tragic*, he painfully revealed as: *'I react very much like a cat or a tiger would react. I look at things more a matter of whether or not it is a threat to me rather than what somebody else's social status is or whatever'* (Stebbing, 2002). Like many adult survivors of childhood sexual abuse, Dennis seemed to lack efficient self-soothing strategies that depend upon a well-developed frontal cortex, the self-regulatory part of the brain.

Research shows that brain development in infancy is mainly experience-dependent. While a nurturing early environment promotes healthy neural development, adverse childhood experiences increase the stress hormone cortisol to such a critical level that it washes over the child's brain like acid (DeMaria *et al*, 1999). It corrodes the frontal cortex, which is so vital in regulating powerful emotions and recognising the trauma as a memory

that only resides in the past.[21] Thus, severe and unpredictable stress on the tender brain impacts information processing, distorts social and chronological perception and keeps the individual stuck in a state of permanent alert. So, long after the threat has gone, the victim remains stuck in the nightmare of the past. In short, the survivor of childhood sexual abuse experiences current stressors with an emotional intensity that belongs to a former time (Streeck-Fischer & van der Kolk, 2000). It is as if early trauma burns lessons in the child's memories, shapes the architecture of his brain and hard wires it to see all subsequent relationships as potentially dangerous.

Shattered sense of self

For Dennis, time stood still. Like many victims of abuse, he was imprisoned by his childhood fears, bound to that which wounded him. In his last televised interview, when asked how much of becoming a cat was part of coming to terms with his difficult childhood, and *'in a way recovering from it'*, Dennis replied, *'I don't know. The bottom line is I had to find my own way and I did'* (Dolan, 2010). And so he found refuge in fantasy, in the murky region between animal and man. The Cat persona protected his immature wounded self from threats, but it kept him cut off from human relatedness.

Like Dennis, the child forced to bond traumatically with his aggressor disowns aspects of his self and surrenders all control to a formidable fantasy figure. This is a desperate psychological survival defence born out of fear, not out of choice. However, once he has been invited in, this Omnipotent Self takes over the inner world and quickly builds emotional contact boundaries that protect the child against further potential hurt, rejection or humiliation. This is a relief for the terrified child, as through this alliance he gains the illusion of safety, believing his powerful new-found saviour will protect him against the evil of the world. But this is nothing more than a Faustian

---

[21] The sombre fact is that this region of the brain is 20–30 per cent smaller in abused children than in children raised in a nurturing environment.

bargain, for his survival has been purchased at an extravagant price: the inability to live a full and creative life. The Omnipotent Self initially provides a source of comfort for the frightened child and allows him to survive emotional starvation and intense distress, but in exchange he demands total control, forbids relational needs, hinders creative living, prevents autonomy and finally contaminates all that gives meaning to life (Taransaud, 2011). In other words, the abusive relational dynamics the individual endured in his early years get replayed internally. It is as if the original abuser now rules from within, keeping the more vulnerable and immature aspects of the self emotionally starved and in a state of frozen terror. Mollon comments that survivors of child sexual abuse tend to inhabit the version of reality presented by their abuser: *'Such vision may include the illusion that the abuser will always have control over the victim'* (2001, p216).

Rip cat-man

The legend of the Windigo tells that although the vulnerable novice possessed by the spirit of the monster adopts attributes of the beast and becomes feral in appearance, deep down remnants of his humanity still persist. He retains enough awareness to know that his behaviour goes against the tribe's moral system, but powerless, and overcome by shame, he often contemplates suicide as the only way out of his misery. Similarly for the abused child, the effect of overwhelming threat on the developing brain not only contributes to a distorted sense of self, promotes aggressive and self-destructive behaviour and compromises the ability to shake off negative thoughts, it also leaves him more vulnerable to severe depression and suicidal thoughts in adulthood (Mendel, 1994).[22]

---

[22] The research shows that in the UK,
- On average, every 22 minutes a teenager tries to kill him- or herself (Institute of Public Policy Research, 2006).
- Suicide remains the leading cause of death for men between 20 and 34 (Davies, 2015).
- The number of suicides registered in 2013 was 6,233. This corresponds to a rate of 11.9 per 100,000 (Samaritans, 2015).
- Victims of childhood sexual abuse are more than twice as likely to attempt suicide (Dube *et al*, 2005).

Dennis escaped into a world of fantasy, but he did not find his way back home and never found acceptance among humankind. Defeated by an existence devoid of solace, he took his own life at the age of 54. His body was discovered in his trailer on Monday 5 November 2012. The words of Albert Camus come to mind: '*How hard it must be to live only with what one knows and what one remembers, cut off from what one hopes for*' (1947, p225).

Conclusion

Dennis's cat persona originated from a violation of trust and power that not only shattered his sense of self and safety but also the boundaries that separate the real from the fantasy. Terrorised, dehumanised and dispossessed of his selfhood, Dennis surrendered his humanity to the fantasy of the abuser. Like the Native American novice indelibly marked by the spirit of the Windigo, his body became a sacrificial altar, an enduring display of the savage abuse he suffered. But maybe the permanent markings were also a form of communication, wordless declarations of the brutal body violations he endured in his early years. His way of expressing what he could not put into words. Dennis's metamorphosis might also have been an attempted form of healing through violent and self-destructive means (Milia, 2000), a desperate effort to regain a sense of mastery and reclaim his body as his own after the abuse. Yet contrary to popular belief, time does not heal all wounds, as his tragic ending shows.

In his fantasy novel *The Name of the Wind* (2007), Patrick Rothfuss writes about the four doors through which we move in order to deal with pain. The first door is the door of sleep, which only allows brief respite for wake always follows. Second is the door of forgetting, but as discussed in chapter 1, the mind resists suppression: whatever we push down the basement of our psyche will eventually resurface. The third door is the one that allows us to leave reality behind and escape into otherness, but prolonged escapism leads to isolation and fragmentation. The Last is the door of death.

Where there is life there will always be pain, and regardless of our efforts we cannot escape it, but we can work through it and heal. And to heal their emotional wounds and reawaken their attachment needs, adolescents, even the most vilely behaved ones, require and deserve tenderness and compassion (Batmanghelidjh, 2013). For love is the healing agent that can warm the frightened and wounded self back to life. But in order to do that, first we need to have an understanding of the complex and difficult developmental processes that adolescents must go through in order to develop their autonomic self and achieve independence. In the following chapter we will turn our attention to a different kind of fictional half-man, half-beast creature, the 21st-century superstar, the Superhero, and more particularly the golden boy of Hollywood, the amazing Spider-Man.

REFERENCES

Batmanghelidjh C (2013) *Mind the Child*, Penguin Books, London.

Bettelheim B (1976) *The Uses of Enchantment: The Meaning and Importance of Fairy Tales.* Peregrine Books, Suffolk.

Camus A (2002) *The Plague*, Penguin Classics, London (first published in 1947).

Daily Mail (2008) Cat Man the Human 'Tiger'. UK 2008.

Davies C (2015) 'Number of suicides in UK increases, with male rate highest since 2001', *The Guardian*, 19th February, 2015.

DeMaria R, Weeks G, &, Hof L (1999) *Focused Genograms: Intergenerational Assessment of Andividuals, Couples, and Families*, Brunner Routledge, East Sussex.

Dolan M (2010) *The World's Strangest Plastic Surgery and Me*, Channel 4, London, UK.

Dube SR, Anda RF, Whitfield CL, Brown DW, Felitti VJ, Dong M, & Giles WH (2005) 'Long-term consequences of childhood sexual abuse by gender of victim', *American Journal of Preventive Medicine*, 28 (5), pp430–8.

Gilmore D (2003) *Monsters: Evil Beings, Mythical Beasts, and All Manner of Imaginary Terrors*, University of Pennsylvania Press, Philadelphia.

Speechmark ⑤

Guggenbuhl-Craig A (1971) *Power in the Helping Professions*, Spring Publications, Dallas, TX.

Institute of Public Policy Research (2006) Citing Hawton K, Houston K, Shepperd R 'Suicide in young people, study of 174 cases, aged under 25 years, based on coroners' and medical records', *British Journal of Psychiatry*, 175, pp271–6.

Kenton E (1932) *Island of Lost Souls*, Paramount Pictures, Los Angeles, CA.

Larratt S (2012) RIP Stalking Cat. Body Modification Ezine. http://news.bme. com/2012/11/12/rip-stalking-cat

Mendel MP (1994) *The Male Survivor: The Impact of Sexual Abuse*, Sage Publications, Thousand Oaks, CA.

Milia D (2000) *Self Mutilation and Art Therapy: Violent Creation*, Jessica Kingsley, London.

Mollon P (2001) *Releasing the Self: The Healing Legacy of Heinz Kohut*, Whurr Publishers, London.

Potts A (2007) *The Mark of the Beast Published in Knowing Animals*, edited by Simmons L & Armstrong P. Brill publishing, Boston, MA.

Rothfuss P (2007) *The Name of the Wind*, Gollancz, London.

Samaritans (2015) Suicide Statistic Report 2015.

Stebbing P (2002) *Animal Tragic*, Channel 5 & First Circle Films, UK.

Streeck-Fischer A & van der Kolk B (2000) 'Down will come baby, cradle and all: diagnostic and therapeutic implications of chronic trauma on child development', *Australian and New Zealand Journal of Psychiatry*, 34 (6), pp903–18.

Taransaud D (2011) *You Think I'm Evil: Practical Strategies for Working with Aggressive and Challenging Adolescents*, Worth Publishing, London.

Wieland S (1998) *Techniques and Issues in Abuse-Focused Therapy with Children and Adolescents: Addressing the Internal Trauma*, Sage Publications, Thousand Oaks, CA.

11

PUBERTY, THE ULTIMATE SPIN

I am dragged along by a strange new force.
Desire and reason are pulling in different directions.
I see the right way and approve it, but follow the wrong.

Ovid

(*Metamorphoses*, AD 8)

In August 1962, comic book legends Stan Lee and Steve Ditko introduced Spider-Man to the world as the first teenaged, masked crime-fighter to occupy a central role in the superhero realm. The Webslinger is a mighty rescuer whose personal life outside of the blue-and-red suit is almost as dramatic and as demanding as the one he faces while in costume. When he is not shooting spider webs or single-handedly battling larger-than-life supervillains, he is Peter Parker, an awkward teenager tormented by school bullies and ridiculed by girls while struggling to hold down a weekend job. He is the most human superhero, and beyond the webbed-wonder hyperbolic tales of heroic exploits are real dramas that mirror the trials of adolescence individuation.

Puberty: here comes the spider-teen

Based on Lee's graphic novel, the Spider-Man trilogy directed by Sam Raimi is an epic tale of Kafkaesque metamorphosis. In the opening sequence of Raimi's first instalment, Peter's voice-over begins with '*Who am I? You sure you wanna to know? The story of my life is not for the faint of heart*'. The dramatic narration can be interpreted as a reminder of the central developmental task of adolescence, which is the pursuit of individuation, to give birth to one's true self, shed old familial ties and emerge as an individual who is distinct from parental object representations.

Every superhero has an origin story and Peter Parker's transformation into Spider-Man represents a period of our youth which most of us can identify

with: puberty. Orphaned at a young age, Peter lives in a modest home with his elderly and impoverished Aunt May and Uncle Ben. An unpopular and wimpy-looking science whiz and a painfully shy grade-A geek, nobody is more surprised than Peter when he wakes up one morning, having been bitten by a genetically engineered spider, to find himself totally transformed. He cries out, '*What's happening to me? I feel different! As though my entire body is charged with some sort of fantastic energy!*' (Lee & Ditko, 1962). Puny Parker is no more. Overnight, his boyish appearance drastically changed; in the place of his once-frail body is now a more muscular physique, hair has grown in strange new places and he no longer needs his glasses; he will never look at the world in the same way again. And that's just the beginning. Peter goes through a '*big change*' as he enthusiastically remarks after a significant downward glance at himself. His sexual awakening coincides with his sudden crush on girl-next-door Mary Jane and is further demonstrated by his new-found ability to produce sticky white fluid with the flick of his wrist (as well as his wish for privacy while he secretly practices his *web-shooting* skills in his bedroom). The spider bite has triggered Peter's puberty, something that has not escaped the notice of his Uncle Ben, who now remarks that Peter is a typical teenager with '*raging hormones*'.

It's not long before our teen hero turns into a daredevil thrill-seeker. He leaps from rooftops and free falls towards the tarmac before swinging into action at the last possible second. Spider-Man's daring acrobatics and death-defying stunts parallel the risk-taking and sensation-seeking behaviour of many adolescents. For example, in June 2014, during national Drowning Prevention Week, a bare-chested teen climbed on top of the curved arch of the 50-foot-high Lowry Bridge in Salford Quays, Manchester, and jumped into the deep icy waters below. When asked why he would risk his life in this way, the teenager replied he simply wanted to '*cool off*'[23] (Readhead, 2014).

---

[23] The boy's plunge was filmed by a passer-by; it can be watched on https://www.youtube.com/watch?v=QzEHkoAOblA&list=PLcl18OaXgJ1vZooXHTKPmTMAd8iM62QUm

Morgan (2005) notes that adolescents base their decisions about risk on how they are feeling at the moment rather than on the consequences of their actions. This is due to the fact that the teenage brain is a work in progress. While the development of the hormone-fuelled limbic system (the part that provides a rewarding feeling after taking a risk) intensifies at the start of puberty, the prefrontal cortex (the thinking and retraining part) does not reach full maturity until a decade later. The mismatch in the timing of the two developments often explains why adolescents have difficulties controlling their impulses and judging risks and rewards (Giedd, 2015). As Addison Allen puts it, *'adolescence is like having only enough light to see the step right in front of you'* (2010, p148).

Regression: the spider crawls back

While the first instalment of Raimi's trilogy illustrates the discovery of new powers, beliefs and identity, *Spider-Man 2* (2004) deals with regression, an integral part of progressive development and psychic restructuring central to the individuation process during puberty (Blos, 1974). Like the average adolescent who in his pursuit of self-discovery tries out different personae, Peter hides behind his mask and experiments with new behaviours while managing to avoid exposure. The mask protects his fragile and unformed developing self, leaving him free to challenge the existing order and operate outside the authorities that have shaped his life to date. In short, the anonymity of the Spidey Suit allows him to safely explore his new abilities, test out his new powers and pursue his own quest for selfhood. But the search for a self of one's own is a painful process. Individuation is a lonely labyrinthine course that only advances via the detour of regression, and it is a pathway littered with the forgotten memorabilia of childhood. Jones (1948) states that regression takes place during puberty where the adolescent recapitulates and expends the development he passed through during his infancy. This strenuous psychological journey that, to some extent, mirrors the early separation-individuation process that takes place in early childhood (and later during midlife), is a necessary step in the journey towards adulthood.

Speechmark

Set two years after Peter reached puberty, *Spider-Man 2* explores Peter's difficulties in balancing both his day-to-day life and that of the web-slinging teen superhero. Based on Lee's classic *Spider-Man No More* (1967), the film starts with Peter narrating, '*I made a choice once to live a life of responsibility … Who am I? I am Spider-Man*'. Yet living a life of responsibility and being an unbending paragon of righteousness weighs Peter down to the point that he wishes to escape and leave behind the demands of his burgeoning adulthood. Entangled in the sticky web of complex physiological, sexual and psychological changes, Peter casts off his heroic mantle and resigns from the superhero business. In a memorable scene, with a backdrop of a storm brewing on the horizon, a disheartened Peter Parker is shown walking away from a garbage bin which now contains his Spider-Man costume. He simply wants to return to a more simple and carefree life that existed before puberty and the spider bite and recover the innocence and childhood he lost. After all, the life of a superhero, like the journey of adolescence, is a lonely and arduous one. As Peter laments, '*if somebody said it was a happy little tale … somebody lied*'. His words echo those of the English playwright and novelist William Somerset Maugham: '*It is an illusion that youth is happy, an illusion of those who have lost it; but the young know they are wretched for they are full of the truthless ideal which have been instilled into them, and each time they come in contact with the real, they are bruised and wounded […]. They must discover for themselves that all they have read and all they have been told are lies, lies, lies*' (1915, p135).

But of course, we don't need to be Peter Parker to experience the traumas of puberty. For many, it involves a rapid transition from a state of comfort and familial security to a place where we no longer feel we belong. Alone and confused, crushed by the complexities of life, we stumble through a minefield of emotions, clumsily negotiating our way between memories of the past and uncertainties about the future, while wondering who we are and what we are going to do with the rest of our lives (Taransaud, 2011). Add to that the stress of examinations, the burden of peer pressure in relation to drugs and sex, an uncontrollable body brimming over with hormones giving rise to ungovernable urges and a not fully developed frontal cortex; it is not surprising that the safety of childhood may appear more desirable.

Frankel notes that adolescents are in 'status nascendi', a state of being born, *'one of the inevitable struggles of adolescence is between a regressive pull back to what is known, familiar and safe, and a forward movement out into the world'* (1998, p6). He advises that our role as adults is not to treat them like children, not to hurry the process by prematurely forcing upon them the burdens of adulthood and not to belittle their struggles by describing what is perhaps the most challenging time of their lives as the best one. Our role is to patiently nurture what is not yet formed and reassure them that the loss of childhood and of one's innocence about the world can be survived.

It is thanks to Aunt May that Peter resumes his superhero duties. Having given away Peter's comic books (the last vestige of his early years), she sets limits, reminds him that *'there is a hero in all of us'* and assists Peter in mourning the loss of his childhood (and his comic book collection) which reignites his heroic quest for individuation. In the ending scene of *Spider-Man 2*, a more mature and confident Peter Parker, dressed in his red-and-blue costume, leaps from his bedroom window, but this is not the end of his struggles. It is not long before our teenage hero is imbued with new powers, provoking another warning from his Uncle Ben, *'you're changing, and that's normal […] Just be careful who you change into'*. Peter's journey towards selfhood is about to take a dramatic new turn.

A descent into darkness

The tag line for *Spider-Man 3* is *'The greatest battle lies … within'*. In this instalment, Peter embarks on a heroic inward journey and discovers that becoming one's own self involves an intimate encounter with the disowned and un-integrated aspects of the psyche.

In the last chapter of the spider-bites-boy saga, our young hero appears to have finally managed to strike a healthy balance between his personal

life and his duties as a costumed crime-fighter. Once more, the film opens with a voice-over by Peter reminding us of his journey so far, '*It's me! Peter Parker! Your friendly neighborhood … You know. I've come a long way from becoming the boy who was bitten by a spider. Back then, nothing seemed to go right for me, and now …*' Well now things are about to get worse for the teenage webbed-wonder as Peter goes for the ultimate spin and suffers a second *super-freaky* mutation. He lets go of his boy-scout attitude and comes face to face with the most fearsome opponent he will ever face – the darker and more primitive aspects of his self, his own Shadow (see chapter 1).

In *A Little Book on the Human Shadow* (1988), Robert Bly describes an invisible bag filled with the parts we have cast aside in order to fit into our immediate environment or gain the approval of others. However, Bly warns that if our Shadow-bag becomes too heavy to carry, a primitive hostile substance starts to leak out and gradually takes hold of us. No doubt Peter has a rather weighty Shadow-bag filled with discarded elements of his life both as a superhero and as a pubescent grade-A student. By being in the public eye, he is constantly under pressure to perform to society's expectations and tenaciously strives to uphold his family motto, '*with great power comes great responsibility*'. But when one side of a polarity gets stretched too far, it is almost automatic that at some point the other side also stretches (Zinker, 1978). One facet of Peter is overemphasised, and it's only a matter of time before an alien symbiote (a creepy-crawly amorphous substance) takes hold of our young hero and transforms the mild-mannered boy-next-door into a vengeful, big-headed glamour-puss and his red-and-blue Spider-Man costume into a slick, black leather suit. And so Peter meets his other half, his dark doppelgänger.

The symbiote erodes Peter's ability to think critically and awakens his darker desires. It feeds off his unexpressed anger, repressed emotions and all that he has suppressed in the process of becoming an epitome of unwavering morality. The shy and nerdy boy looks deep into the abyss and likes what he sees. A whole new world has opened up before him. This new mutation has given him a new kind of awareness that he has never experienced before. Intoxicated by his new powers, he feels invincible. He discards his superhero responsibilities and gives free rein to his teenage impulses and hubristic quest for fame. Our once '*friendly neighbourhood Spider-Man*' lets go of his noble attitude and starts using his superpowers to satisfy his selfish needs. He turns into a pitiless and amoral vigilante with a new motto, '*You want forgiveness? Seek religion*'.

Surviving the tussle

When newly emergent features of the self come into consciousness during adolescence, so does the Shadow, but somewhere inside, something of the securely attached boy-next-door endures. Once again, it is Aunt May who lands a helping hand and brings Peter to a new sense of realisation. She is the embodiment of the archetypal figure Jung calls the Wise Old One.[24] She represents '*knowledge, reflection, insight, wisdom, cleverness and intuition*' and appears when '*insight, understanding, good advice, determination, planning, etc. are needed but cannot be mustered on one's own*' (1959, pp214, 220). In short, her role is to ensure a smooth transition from the old to the new (Stewart, 1998). During a heart-to-heart conversation she offers empathy, guidance and containment, which afford Peter the courage to confront and master his destructive side. He acknowledges the opposing forces within him, reconnects with the parts he had disowned and eventually removes the dark leather suit. He resumes his journey towards adulthood enriched with a far richer connection with himself and his environment.

Peter's intimate encounter with the mysterious alien parasite was key to his emotional growth. It allowed him to reconnect with the parts he had

---

[24] In legends, pop culture and classic literature, the Wise Old One often appears in the shape of a wizard, a mentor, a knowledgeable hermit, a teacher, a grandparent or an ancestral guiding spirit. In youth culture, famous examples of the Wise Old One archetype include Obi-Wan Kenobi and Yoda from *Star Wars*, Albus Dumbledore from *Harry Potter*, Gandalf from *Lord of the Rings*, Professor Xavier from *X-Men*, Jor-El from *Superman*, Alfred the butler from *Batman*, the old woman Oracle from *The Matrix* and Mr. Miyagi from *Karate Kid*.

Speechmark

disowned and move forward with a deeper level of awareness. Perhaps we could say the same about adolescent rebellion – that it, too, is both healthy and necessary. The thirst for forbidden knowledge, to cross the line of familiar boundaries and to stray into unexplored territories may be a perilous venture fraught with many dangers, but it expresses a natural desire to discover one's true self and exist as separate and distinct. As Winnicott confirms, '*if you do all you can to promote personal growth in your offspring, you will need to be able to deal with startling results. If your children find themselves at all they will not be contented to find anything but the whole of themselves, and that will include the aggression and destructive elements in themselves as well as the elements that can be labeled loving*' (1971, p193). Winnicott also stresses the importance of the adult surviving the '*tussle*' that might ensue '*without changing colour, without relinquishment of any important principle*' (1971, p196) but by maintaining an empathic yet assertive stance in setting boundaries within which the adolescent can safely explore his destructive urges. And like Peter, the adolescent will also need a compassionate Wise Old One (often outside the immediate family) with whom he can share and reflect upon his experiences. For as we discussed in chapters 5 and 6, confronting the alienated aspects of the self is not a solitary endeavour; it requires the presence of a caring witness.

Drawing upon the work of Campbell (1949), Mike Alsford points out that '*the myth of the hero confronts us with the challenge of transformation, the call to develop, to progress, to grow up by freeing ourselves from the limitations of infancy*' (2006, p3). And this is precisely what Peter did. Not only has he vanquished his most terrifying opponent, he has also resolved his inner conflicts. He has reconciled his instinctual nature, the lessons he learned in his childhood and his newly developed urges for novel experiences within the realities of life. The teenage Webslinger has reached spiritual maturity. He has become a Man.

As for the alien symbiote, it does not die but finds a new host called Eddie Brock, a broken-hearted journalist who has had more than his share of bad luck in life. Unlike Peter, who grew up in a safe and loving environment, Eddie was raised by a cold and unloving father who blamed him for his wife's death during childbirth (Michelinie, 1993). The profound shame and loss Eddie experienced throughout his childhood left a deep psychological wound which becomes a fertile soil for infection by predatory organisms and a tasty treat for the symbiote. The dark amorphous substance leeches onto him, feeds off his childhood untended hurt and unlocks his immature rage. Consumed by the parasitic life, Eddie surrenders to an irreversible bestial metamorphosis. He abandons all control, hands over his wounded immature Self to this dark entity and emerges as the powerful and fearless supervillain Venom, a far cry from the way he was made to feel in his early years. In short, without sufficient self-support and environmental support to confront his shadow and learn from it, he identifies with it.

Conclusion

A humorous parable illustrates the trials of adolescent individuation. It tells the story of a gifted healer who passed by a blind man and restored his sight. He later saw another man who was possessed by a demon and set him free. Then the healer saw a man crying. When he asked about his problem, the man replied he was the father of a teenager. All the healer could do was sit down and weep with him. As Winnicott notes, '*the cure for adolescence belongs to the passage of time and to the gradual maturation processes [...] The process cannot be hurried or slowed up*' (1965, p115); it must be suffered and lived through.

The rapid physiological, biological and psychological changes that come about at the start of puberty seem to parallel those of the young fictional superhero as he gains his superpowers and increases in potency. The struggles of these mighty fantasy characters resonate very deeply with many of today's adolescents who find echo in their inner worlds. They mirror their internal conflicts, their illusions of omnipotence and their pursuits of individuation. They attest to their wish to escape into alterity, explore their

destructive side, confront their newly developed urges and eventually find the hero within. But, as we will explore in the next chapter, for the antisocial teen who never had the opportunity to heal his childhood wounds, the righteous superhero has no appeal. Instead he is more likely to identify with the villain, the evil mastermind who seeks prestige, power and limelight and whose behaviour is motivated by revenge and, of course, fear.

REFERENCES

Addison Allen S (2010) *The Girl Who Chased the Moon*, Random House, New York.

Alsford M (2006) *Heroes and Villains*, Alsford Darton, Longman & Todd Ltd., London.

Blos P (1974) *The Young Adolescent: Clinical Studies*, Free Press, New York.

Bly R (1988) *A Little Book on the Human Shadow*, Harper Collins, New York.

Campbell J (2008) *The Hero with a Thousand Faces*, New World Library, Novato, CA (first published in 1949).

Frankel R (1998) *The Adolescent Psyche: Jungian and Winnicottian Perspectives*, Routledge, London.

Giedd J (2015) 'The amazing teen brain', published in *Scientific American*, Vol. 312. New York; June 2015.

Jones E (1948) *Some Problems of Adolescence*. In Papers on Psycho-Analysis. Bailliere, Tidal & Cox, London.

Jung C (1990) *The Archetypes and the Collective Unconscious, Vol. 9*, Princeton University Press, New York (first published in 1959).

Lee S & Ditko S (1962) *Spider-Man* published in *Amazing Fantasy, Vol. 15*, Marvel Comics, New York.

Lee S & Ditko S (1967) *Spider-Man No More*, published in The Amazing Spiderman, Vol. 1. Marvel Comics, New York.

Michelinie D (1993) *Venom, Lethal Protector*, Marvel Comics, New York.

Morgan N (2005) *Blame My Brain: The Amazing Teenage Brain Revealed*, Walkers Books, London.

Ovid (2004) *Metamorphoses*, Book VII. Penguin Classics, London (written in AD 8).

Raimi S (2002, 2004, 2007) *Spiderman Trillogy*, Columbia Pictures, Culver City, CA.

Readhead H (2014) 'Teenager jumps 50ft from bridge into canal because he wanted to cool off', *Metro*, 24th June 2014.

Somerset Maugham W (2006) *Of Human Bondage*, Random House, New York (first published in 1915).

Stewart W (1998) *Dictionary of Images and Symbols in Counselling*, Jessica Kingsley, London.

Taransaud D (2011) *You Think I'm Evil: Practical Strategies for Working with Aggressive and Challenging Adolescents*, Worth Publishing, London.

Winnicott D (2005) *Playing and Reality: Contemporary Concepts of Adolescent Development and Their Implications for Higher Education*, Routledge, New York (first published in 1971).

Winnicott DW (2006) *The Family and Individual Development*, Routledge, Oxon (first published in 1965).

Zinker J (1978) *Creative Process in Gestalt Therapy*, Vintage Books, New York.

12

THE RAGE TO FEEL ALIVE

*But you know what scares me the most? When I can't fight it
anymore, when it takes over, when I totally lose control …
I like it.*

Bruce Banner, aka the Hulk, played by Eric Bana
(Ang Lee. *Hulk*, Universal Pictures, 2003)

In the late 1930s, during the rise of Nazism and in the midst of the Holocaust,
two 17-year-old Jewish teenagers, Jerry Siegel and Joe Shuster, found
refuge in fantasy and together created the first costumed superhero – the
Man of Steel – Superman. The story of the last son of Krypton, rocketed to
earth to escape the destruction of his birth planet and later adopted by the
loving Martha and Jonathan Kent, resonated loudly among the millions of
American Jews in the early 1940s and those who managed to escape from
German-occupied Europe. The popularity of Superman was such, and the
demand for fantasy so great, that during World War Two, over 30 per cent of
printed materials shipped to military bases were comic books. But, post-1945,
superhero comic book sales plunged by 75 per cent (Carter, 2010). The war
was over and the world felt safe again; it appeared that fictional rescuers
were no longer needed.

But now they are back. For the past decade, they have dominated
multimedia and powered up to the top of international box-office
blockbusters. This recent superhero-mania began only a few weeks after
the tragic events that shook the world on 11 September 2001. Once again,
the world did not feel safe, and we allowed the superheroes to flex their
way back into our imagination. As Packer confirms, *'superheroes rise in
popularity when times are tougher and when hopes have been dashed […]
When reality fails, fantasy is always in the wings, ready to come to the
rescue'* (2010, pp48–9).

The entertainment industry understands our needs for escapism. In times of uncertainty or mental torment, most of us seek refuge in fantasy and wish we could be more than we already are. These occasional flights into fantasy are necessary for our psychological equilibrium. They briefly relieve us from the burden of painful thoughts and momentarily appease many of the stresses in our lives. There is nothing wrong with temporary escapes and brief, idle daydreaming, as long as we do not conspire with our soothing and sometimes distorted reveries. For this is the danger with prolonged escapism; it can become a permanent anaesthetic, causing us to sleepwalk through life, thus cutting us off from reality, an ad hoc coping strategy that many love-starved children adopt to withstand emotional pain and survive hostile relational environments.

Emotional orphans

As previously discussed, the journey of the superhero has strong parallels with that of the securely attached adolescent on his quest towards individuation. However, it is the superhero's counterpart that broadens and deepens our understanding of the inner world of the troubled teen. For far beneath the rigidly worn masks of the fictional supervillain lies a deep hurt, a painful emotional wound and the shamed, frightened self of his early years.

An exploration of these characters' origins reveals that heroes and villains share a common history. Both have experienced traumatic incidents in their early years, often loss, deprivation or abandonment and at times even abuse and torture. However, in spite of his painful past, the hero can celebrate his duality. For example, Superman effortlessly reverses time by flying at superhuman speed around the earth and turns into a mild-mannered reporter as soon as he puts on his glasses. He is able to emerge from nerdy obscurity to battle evil villains, to fluidly move from ordinary to super, to go from his 'fortress of solitude' to the social world and to quickly move from the world of power and infinite possibilities to the world of quotidian reality (Browne & Fiswick, 1983). In other words, like the securely attached adolescent who has

Speechmark Ⓢ

confronted the opposing forces within him and resolved his inner conflicts, he is able to live a full and creative life, adapting his behaviour to any given situation.

On the contrary, the villain does not have that luxury; his journey resembles that of the emotionally wounded teen. Unlike his securely attached counterpart he never had the opportunity to merge with the love and warmth of a good-enough other, work through his traumatic experiences and heal his childhood wounds. So, while the hero experiences relationships between a multitude of polar opposites, the antisocial villain remains stuck at one end of the continuum, bound to a fantasy super-world where only the strongest survives. In short, and to paraphrase the famous quote from the German philosopher Nietsche (1889), what did not kill the hero and made him stronger jostled the wounded villain onto a dark track found its way inside and took over the fragile and developing self. Or, as Batman's arch-enemy, the Joker, says, '*I believe whatever doesn't kill you, simply makes you ... stranger*'[25] (Nolan, 2008).

To illustrate this point, let's briefly return to the inveterate protector of the oppressed, America's first superhero, Superman. In spite of his tragic start in life, Superman grew up to view our world as a predominantly safe and stable place, where people are generally caring and reliable. Thanks to the love and warmth he received from his adoptive parents, he became an individual able to live a full and creative existence while devoting his life to the benefit of humankind. But let's explore a 'what if' scenario for the Man of Steel as illustrated by award-winning writer Kurt Busiek in the comic book *Camelot Falls 1* (2006). Let's imagine that having barely escaped the destruction of his home planet and having drifted alone through hyperspace, Superman's tiny spaceship had landed in the middle of a war zone rather than the vast wheat field in Smallville, Kansas. And let's pretend that instead of being

---

[25] Max Sugar confirms the Joker's statement: '*When confronted with the feeling of being a stranger to oneself and to others, and being unable to use coping strategies from childhood, a crisis may develop which destabilizes the individual's self system*' (1999, p254).

---

rescued and adopted by the loving Ma' and Pa' Kent, he was locked in a cage by heartless soldiers and sadistic scientists, kept alive but sedated and cruelly experimented on for decades. What would he have become? Would he still have emerged as the caped crusader fighting for '*truth, justice and the American way*'? Probably not. More likely, he would have developed into a twisted version of the Man of Steel, a vengeful and wounded villain traumatised by childhood losses, quick to anger and hell-bent on disrupting social order. His reality would have been very different from ours. Like many adolescents who have experienced first-hand emotional and physical abuse, this Superman would have been raised to believe that our world is nothing more than a hostile place, populated by heartless and malevolent people. He would have been taught that in such a merciless Darwinian world, the most powerful always sits on top of the food chain, and that survival depends on being king among beasts. In the absence of love, warmth and safety, Superman would have learned to rely on a substitute in the form of power, domination and aggression.

In this light, it is easy to see why such fictional characters have a personal resonance for the child brought up in an environment that is cold and oppressive. Emotionally starved, trapped by a sense of hopelessness and without any external source to provide for his basic needs, he seeks refuge in fantasy and learns to rely on a mighty omnipotent self, a domineering facade that hides any trace of vulnerability. This alliance with an all-powerful saviour redresses the child's feelings of inadequacy and allows him to survive in a world he perceives as dangerous and cruel. Sadly, this coping strategy also obscures his view of the world and cuts him off from sources of support and emotional closeness. For this omnipotent self does not allow for love. He's always on his guard, and any breach in the relative sense of security he has established triggers an immediate protective aggressive response (Taransaud, 2011), as depicted by the most angry character in the Marvel Universe, the incredible Hulk (Lee & Kirby, 1962).

The gamma ray-spawned freak

So far, we have discussed the flawless superhero and his arch-enemy, the notorious supervillain. Let's now turn our attention to a third type of super pop icon: the flawed and angry superhero.[26] Arguably, one of the most popular is the incredible Hulk, a heavy-browed half-man, half-beast giant recently described as '*a man with breathtaking anger management issues*' (Whedon, 2012).

Like many troubled teens, the Hulk is perceived as an uncontrollable lawless savage by the authorities who wish to put the 'beast' down or at least keep it caged. Originally inspired by the narratives of both Frankenstein and Dr Jekyll and Mr Hyde (DeFalco, 2003), the graphic novel and, more recently, the Ang Lee movie (2003) tell the story of Dr Bruce Banner. Bruce is an introverted and intellectually gifted scientist who, after an accidental overexposure to gamma radiation, involuntarily transforms into an eight-foot-tall raging green behemoth every time he is under emotional stress. However, all is not what it seems. Contrary to most villains, Banner is aware of opposing forces within himself; yet unlike the hero, he is unable to regulate powerful affective states. In other words, similar to the child deprived of appropriate maternal care, he doesn't possess the necessary tools to monitor his emotional responses and soothe himself (see chapter 14). Instead, he channels intense emotions, such as fear, shame and anger, by unleashing the gamma ray-spawned freak and smashing everything that stands in his way.

An exploration of his youth reveals painful psychological traumas and a childhood tainted by both loss and fear. After a difficult birth, Bruce grew up in a violent home and suffered daily abuse at the hands of an alcoholic

---

[26] Masters defines the flawed anti-hero as a tortured rebel, a doer of good with considerable damage. He '*exhibits some of the qualities associated with the villain, ranging from brutality to cynicism to an apparent lack of empathy, yet is capable of taking heroic action*' (2015, p133). Other popular angry superheroes include Wolverine (James Howlett/Logan), X-23 (Laura Kinney), Rorschach (Walter Joseph Kovacs) and the Thing (Benjamin Jacob Grimm).

father who ended up in a psychiatric institute after murdering Bruce's mother. Banner's early history furthers our understanding of the survival strategies a child employs when the people who are supposed to keep him safe and provide for his needs are the cause of his distress. When the source of danger happens to live at home, the terrified child, incapable of physically fighting his way out of the situation or running away from his hostile environment, regresses into fearful submission and plays dead. Unable to discharge the powerful fight-or-flight survival energy locked in by the freezing response, his system remains stuck in survival mode, in a constant state of readiness and reactivity (Levine, 1997).

So, contrary to popular belief, the gamma rays are not responsible for the Hulk's unstoppable rage. As Banner reveals, '*The gamma just unleashed what was already there*' (Lee, 2003). They amplified and unlocked the hurt buried deep within his psyche and released the frustrated fight-or-flight energies bound up in his nervous system since childhood. So whenever Banner is exposed to cues that resemble aspects of his original trauma, the enraged beast takes over, avenging the grievous injustice of the past with deadly force.

Again, like the antisocial adolescent, this fictional green monster is not just a mindless savage; he is a wounded survivor and a misunderstood outcast unleashing his hurt whenever he is reminded of the unbearable feelings of insecurity and vulnerability he experienced in his early years. His rage is not the rage of a monster but that of a vulnerable, frightened and helpless child. It is the rage to feel alive.

Trapped in the legacy of his past, Bruce Banner survives by living in shadows, is suspicious of everybody and deeply mistrustful of intimacy. His only attachment figure is Dr Betty Ross, a childhood friend and co-researcher. But although Betty is an ordinary woman, she has an extraordinary power; she has the ability to empathise with Bruce's fears, validate the raw energy of the Hulk, break through the rage and safely access the vulnerable core. She

sees the hurt child within the beast. So this raises a question: what kind of superpowers do we need to support our so-called 'villainous' teens? Again, the deceptively formulaic narratives within the superhero genre provide us with some answers.

In superhero fantasy, the villain spends much of his time plotting to eliminate the hero whom he regards as the main obstacle to his ultimate grandiose goal: world domination. However, when he finally has the hero at his mercy, dangling above a vat of acid or a shark-filled tank, he doesn't cut the rope; instead, he delivers a long-winded autobiographical monologue, boasting about his greatness and disclosing his evil master plan (and sometimes aspects of his tragic past), while the hero invariably wriggles his way out of the situation. Why does he regale the hero with his life story and let him into his secrets? Perhaps the villain seeks the approval of the hero and envies him for being able to conquer his early traumatic experiences and heal his wounds. Perhaps he hopes that the emotionally healthy superhero will see beyond the curtains of evilness and, like a 'good-enough Mother' (Winnicott, 1971), will facilitate his omnipotent fantasies, fulfil his unmet infantile emotional needs for love and acceptance and support him in rediscovering the hidden potential that lies beneath his antisocial behaviour. But the villain's monologue always remains one-sided; it never turns into a dialogue. His failure to become visible in the eyes of a compassionate other keeps him stuck in the past, re-enacting internally and externally his early traumatic experiences.

Conclusion

At one time or another, most of us have imagined what it would be like to have superpowers. Between 2006 and 2008, the Syfy (formerly Sci-Fi Channel) presented a weekly reality series *Who wants to be a Superhero?* Hosted by the comic book legend, Stan Lee, 11 participants were invited to satisfy their lust for fame and live their fantasies by moving into a secret lair, dressing up as their own superhero alter ego and competing against each other for the ultimate geek price: immortalisation in a comic book. Some of us may perceive these contestants as desperate wannabes or social misfits locked in their childhood fantasies. Yet, if we are truly honest with ourselves, the real answer to *who wants to be a Superhero* is: most of us do! And so we should. As the next part of this book's focus will reveal, to support antisocial teens in re-engaging flexibly with life and expand their behavioural options, we must walk the hero's path. We must venture out from our known world into the perceptual world of the troubled youth, follow the trail to where things went wrong, engage with the 'wild things' that lurk within, find their untapped potential and allow ourselves to be moved and transformed by our journey. And although this might seem like an insurmountable task, we can take comfort in Aunt May's wisdom: '*There's a hero in all of us*' (Raimi, 2004). We may not have X-ray vision, but if we dare to look beneath the omnipotent persona of the challenging teen, we will see evidence of a painful past and a frightened self that is still crying out for the life for which he has been deprived. Similarly, we do not need mind-reading powers to ascertain that his behaviour is a form a communication, an SOS distress call, an infantile yearning for environmental stability. We might not have super strength, yet in chapter 16 we will see that we can be robust enough to face his persecutory inner figures and simultaneously vulnerable enough to invite a meaningful relationship and build a strong and healing working alliance. And although we might not be able to reverse time, in chapters 17 and 18, we will discover that through the arts we can go back to the moment of deprivation and provide him with new and healthier responses. But perhaps most importantly, we will discover that unlike the Marvel heroes, we do not need a cape, a shiny spandex costume or a secret identity; we just need to keep an open mind from an informed position and be authentic and self-aware – for being ourselves is heroic enough.

However, before we dig deep into the approach we need to adopt to access the true potential of the wounded youth, let's further our understanding of this omnipotent self and look at it from a different perspective. The following

Speechmark

case study highlights that irrespective of his behaviour, the adolescent's needs to maintain a controlling and domineering attitude ought to be respected and deserve acknowledgement; after all, his alliance with an all-powerful and omnipotent self is what initially helped him survive in a very dangerous world.

REFERENCES

Browne R & Fiswick M (1983) *Hero in Transition*, Popular Press, Bowling Green, OH.

Busiek K (2006) *Camelot Falls*, DC Comics, New York.

Carter M (2010) *Secret Origin: The Secret of DC Comics*, DC Entertainment, New York.

DeFalco T (2003) *Hulk, The Incredible Guide*, Dorling Kindersley, London.

Lee A (2003) *Hulk*, Universal Pictures, Universal City, CA.

Lee S & Kirby J (1962) *The Incredible Hulk*, Marvel Comics, New York.

Levine P (1997) *Waking the Tiger: Healing Trauma*, North Atlantic Books, Berkeley, CA.

Masters AR (2015) *To Be a Man*, Sounds True, Boulder, CO.

Nietsche F (2003) *The Twilight of the Idols*, Penguin Books, London (first published in1889).

Nolan C (2008) *The Dark Knight*, Warner Bros, Burbank, CA.

Packer S (2010) *Superheroes and Superegos*, Praeger, Santa Barbara, CA.

Raimi S (2004) *Spiderman 2*, Columbia Pictures, Culver City, CA.

Sugar M (1999) *Trauma and Adolescence*, International Universities Press, Madison, CT.

Syfy (2006–2008) *Who Wants to be a Superhero*, Nash Entertainment, Los Angeles, CA.

Taransaud D (2011) *You Think I'm Evil: Practical Strategies for Working with Aggressive and Challenging Adolescents*, Worth Publishing, London.

Whedon J (2012) *Avengers Assemble*, Marvel Studios, Burbank, CA.

Winnicott D (2005) *Playing and Reality: Contemporary Concepts of Adolescent Development and Their Implications for Higher Education*, Routledge, New York (first published in 1971).

13

SAVIOUR AND DECEIVER

Tony Stark: *Hey, I've read all about your accident. That much gamma exposure should have killed you.*

Bruce Banner: *So you're saying that the Hulk … the other guy … saved my life? That's nice. It's a nice sentiment.*

(Whedon J. *Avengers Assemble*, Marvel Studios, 2012)

Monty grew up in a violent home. When he turned six his dad passed away and his mother sold the family house and moved to a small apartment with him. As a single mother, disempowered and emotionally exhausted by years of abuse, she often sank into deep depression where she was unable to care for Monty and provide for his physical and emotional needs. During these low periods, household chores were neglected, the fridge remained empty and Monty spent most of his time sitting in front of the TV, babysat by violent video games and action-filled movies. It was only when 10-year-old Monty was caught stealing money to buy his school lunch that his mother was finally offered emotional support and care-giving resources.

The ambiguous Piper

On the first occasion I met up with him, he gave me an eager smile that never reached his eyes, and although he was standing right in front of me, he might as well have not been there at all. Later on, when I met his mother, she confirmed my first impression: '*My son lives with the fairies; his head is always in the clouds*'. Monty was an avid reader of superhero comics and often sought refuge from reality within the small frames of American graphic novels, a fantasy world populated by masked vigilantes, invincible avengers and other testosterone-powered characters; it was also a safe world where there was no room for negative feelings, fear or uncertainties. Monty's favourite superhero was Hartley Rathaway, a social outcast and musical prodigy, also known as the Pied Piper (Broome & Infantino, 1959).

Rathaway-Piper is an ambiguous superhero and reformed criminal pursued by heroes and villains alike who, like his legendary namesake, uses sonic weaponry and mind control to alter perceptions and enslave his enemies.

Monty enjoyed bringing his comics to our sessions, and he was absolutely fascinated by this ambiguous character who could be both a superhero, fighting against evil, and a manipulative minstrel who had not entirely abandoned his former wicked ways. Curious to understand the source of his admiration, I invited him to retrace the steps of the original Pied Piper portrayed in Browning's classic poem (1842).

The Pied Piper of Hamelin tells the story of a shadowy figure who uses his haunting music to drown the rats that plague the town of Hamelin. However, when the townsfolk renege on their promise of payment, the Piper uses his music to lure their children to a cave where they all disappear.

Monty quickly identified with the mysterious rat catcher, took his side and concluded that the villagers deserved the Piper's vengeance. I silently wondered if Monty was trying to tell me something about himself through his fiction. I invited him to take part in a role-play and retell Browning's poem from two different perspectives: Hamelin's children and the Piper. As for me, I would play the role of an impartial journalist eager to find out about the characters' respective experiences and perceptions (we will further explore how to use stories and imaginative play in chapter 21).

To my surprise, Monty chose to begin with the children's point of view. When acting the role of a little boy living in Hamelin, Monty told me how unsafe it was in his town, how he could never play and how in order to survive he had to hide in a wardrobe and stay very still. It was a story of neglect, fear and loneliness, a story in which the child was surrounded by menacing creatures, disease, irresponsible adults and forced to live in deep isolation. He then described the Pied Piper as a foreign visitor dressed in colourful clothes who suddenly appeared out of nowhere to whisk him away from the rat's nest to an enchanted new world. However, Monty quickly lost his spirit, looked down and concluded that it was no better being rescued by this Piper, because now he was simply stuck in a cave, captive in a foreign land with no one to talk to and no hope of return.

After de-roling and providing empathy for the character he had just role-played, I invited Monty to retell the story from the Piper's point of view. He effortlessly presented himself as an enigmatic and powerful wizard sent to Hamelin to free a filthy town from a terrible plague of rats. He reported that when the townsfolk refused to pay for his services, he became enraged; he was furious and blamed the adults for their careless behaviour and for their lack of morality. It was their fault the town was full of rats, and they could not be trusted. He then added it was his duty of care to take the children away from such a terrible place. In Monty's eyes, when the Piper bewitched the children, it was not a premeditated act of revenge or a mass kidnapping but a rescue mission.

So if Browning's infamous rat catcher was on the witness stand, would the jury rule this powerful minstrel as a malicious vigilante and bitter wizard who enticed vulnerable children into a dark dreamland never to be seen again, or would they perceive him as a misunderstood hero who rescued frightened youths from a dangerous and corrupt land plagued by predatory creatures and unreliable adults? After all, the poem intimates that it was not safe to play in Hamelin. In fact, Browning describes their magical new world as a sanctuary, 'a joyous land, [...] where waters gushed and fruit trees grew, and flowers put forth a fairer hue, and everything was strange and new' (1842, p185). Is the Piper innocent or guilty? Saviour or abductor? The answer is not straightforward. After all, as Lapworth et al (1993) notes, some rescuers use their superiority ostensibly to benefit others but simultaneously keep them powerless. However, irrespective of the Piper's intentions – good or bad – there is no denying that the children were trapped in a false paradise by an omnipotent master, free from harm yet cut off from reality, leading a limbo-like existence, stuck in a state of childlike dependency for, perhaps, eternity.

Conclusion

The two versions of Monty's narrative were an accurate representation of his internal cast of characters as well as their interactions. The neglect and the abusive relational dynamics he endured in his early years were now replayed internally, and Monty was dancing to the tune of an inner omnipotent ruler.

Like the ambiguous rat catcher, this internal rescuing figure is both saviour and kidnapper; it provides the frightened and orphaned parts of the self with an inner sanctum free from harm but keeps it captive, confined to an inescapable and impenetrable prison that alienates the child farther from emotional closeness (Taransaud, 2011).

However, we must not forget that this absolute ruler allowed the child to survive emotional starvation. In this sense, unlike the townsfolk who refused to pay the Piper, we should pay him his due and give him some credit for his initial intentions. He is not beyond redemption, and when exposed to a safe, and empathetic environment, his power can be harnessed. He has the potential to become a powerful leader who brings hope, frees the adolescent's captive emotions and helps him find his way back on the road of creative living. For this is the thing with fantasies, although they may lead astray; they are also a door to a renewed and more self-aware self. As Ethel Person puts it, '*Fantasies may serve as consolations, compensations for what we lack in life. They may also heal or undo past wounds, and old conflicts. Perhaps the most compelling function of fantasy is that it creates an ambiance of hope for the future, and gives us the strength to endure*' (1995, p5).

REFERENCES

Broome J & Infantino C (1959) *Flash*, Vol. 106, DC Comics, Manhattan.

Browning R (2009) *The Pied Piper of Hamelin*, published in Bells and Pomegranates. BiblioBazaar, Carolina (first published in 1842).

Lapworth P, Sills C, & Fish S (1993) *Transactional Analysis Counselling*, Speechmark, Oxon.

Person E (1995) *By Force of Fantasy: How We Make Our Lives*, Basic Books, New York.

Taransaud D (2011) *You Think I'm Evil: Practical Strategies for Working with Aggressive and Challenging Adolescents*, Worth Publishing, London.

Whedon J (2012) *Avengers Assemble*, Marvel Studios, Burbank, CA.

Speechmark

PART 3

Healing the hurt

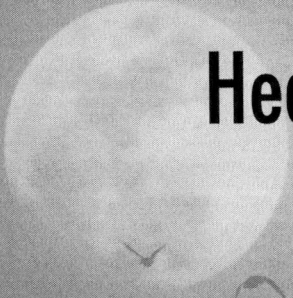

14

MINIBEASTS AND WARMFUZZIES

We need four hugs a day for survival.
We need eight hugs a day for maintenance.
We need twelve hugs a day for growth.

Virginia Satir

On 25 March 2010, first-time parents Kate and David Ogg were told that their baby boy, Jamie, born prematurely at 26 weeks, had stopped breathing. After a team of doctors tried to resuscitate him for 20 minutes, they pronounced the newborn dead and placed his cold, lifeless body on his mother's bare chest so she could grieve and say her goodbyes. Kate instinctively cuddled her child and asked her husband to take off his shirt and climb into the bed to provide extra warmth. They held their son skin-to-skin in a tender embrace for two hours. *'He was on his way out of the world, we wanted for him to know who his parents were and to know that we loved him'*, Kate said. *'Putting him on my chest was the closest he could have been to being inside me where he was last safe [...] We were just trying to make the most of those last precious moments. We wanted to give him as much warmth as we could'* (Michaels, NBC, 2010). Although baby Jamie showed no visible signs of life, he occasionally gasped for air, a natural reflex the doctors had told the Oggs to expect. But Jamie started to gasp more and more regularly and his breathing gradually grew stronger. After two hours he opened his eyes and, to the disbelief of the doctors, he drank a drop of breast milk from his mother. The soft cocooning warmth of his parents had brought him back to life. Hospital personnel rushed back and nursed him to full recovery. Jamie is now a healthy and bouncy six-year-old boy who has not encountered one medical problem since his birth.

In this chapter we will explore how bodily intimacy is essential for postnatal survival and the critical role of touch and holding (both physical and symbolic) in emotional development and healthy neurobiological growth. We will then discuss how empathic holding can warm the wounded self back to life and help adolescents return to creative living. But first let's turn our attention to a new kind of monster. Let's venture into the world of the minibeasts and more particularly that of the desert locust (*Schistocerca gregaria*).

The Jekyll and Hyde of the insect world

The desert locust, bright green in colour, is a reclusive and slow-walking creature that actively avoids other locusts. But this solitary insect displays an extreme form of phenotypic plasticity: it has the ability to alter both its appearance and behaviour in response to changes in its environment. At high density it mutates into a gregarious minibeast, darker in colour, that enjoys the hustle and bustle of community life. Professor Malcolm Burrows, a neurobiologist at the University of Cambridge, identified the stimuli that cause this astonishing shift from solitary to gregarious behaviour (Malone, 2013). In the laboratory, the reclusive locust can be transformed into a highly sociable one by gently stroking its hind legs with a fine paintbrush for a couple of hours. This tactile stimulation, which mimics the jostling it experiences in swarms, activates a chemical hormone also present in the human brain, serotonin, a neurotransmitter that promotes pro-social behaviour when its levels are high and aggression and depression when its levels are low (Fortuna & Knafo, 2014).

The happiness hormone

Serotonin (5-hydroxytryptamine), also known as the 'happiness hormone', is a mood regulator that has been implicated in virtually every aspect of behaviour, such as appetitive, emotional, motor, cognitive and autonomic (Frazer & Hensler, 1999). This neurotransmitter encourages cooperation between the amygdala (the emotional centre of the brain responsible for the fight-or-flight response) and its restraining prefrontal cortex (the rational part of the brain). Not only is serotonin involved in the neural control of expressing aggressive behaviour, but it also brings a sense of security and trust. It

soothes emotional distress, fosters feelings of calm happiness and favours social behaviour. Research shows that low-serotonin individuals exhibit non-cooperative and antagonistic behaviour and are more inclined to depression, suicide ideation, anxiety and aggressive outbursts than high-serotonin individuals (Breuning, 2011).[27]

Touch promotes social bonds

As Professor Burrows and his team uncovered, the change of the locust from solitary to gregarious phase is triggered by a change in its environment. At high density, or when gently held and caressed, the solitary grasshopper transforms into a sociable creature that seeks others. However, the transformation is not permanent; Burrows also discovered that if kept isolated for several hours, the locust will eventually revert back to its hermitlike existence. In other words, if relationships are where things developmentally can go wrong, relationships are also where they can be put right (Howe, 2005). The same applies to humans; we are not so different from the desert locust. Numerous neurobiologists and developmental psychologists who studied the effect of stress on touch-deprived children came to the same conclusion: touch is an essential biological need and is of fundamental importance for the maturation of neural circuits (Bjornsdotter *et al*, 2014). While a lack of physical affirmation has been linked with neurodevelopment problems leading to aggression and fear of intimacy, touch lays the foundation of emotional stability. A loving embrace, a stroke to the arm or a friendly handshake boosts our serotonin level and floods our bodies with oxytocin, a bonding hormone that reduces levels of the stress hormone cortisol and promotes trust. Furthermore, touch is the very first sense we develop in utero and our most developed sensory modality at birth. It is the first language we learn and therefore it plays a key role in

---

[27] After giving volunteers a diet that reduced their serotonin levels, researchers found that the connection between the amygdala and the prefrontal cortex had considerably reduced and impaired the volunteers' capacity to self-soothe as well as their ability to inhibit destructive impulses (Passamonti, 2011).

---

the establishment of a healthy bond between primary caregiver and child (Keltner, 2009). It is critical for healthy cognitive and emotional development and remains crucial for physical and psychological well-being until the day we pass away. As the renowned anthropologist Ashley Montagu emphasises, besides the brain, the skin is the most important of all our organ systems: *'A human being can spend his life blind and deaf and completely lacking the senses of smell and taste, but he cannot survive at all without the functions performed by the skin'* (1971, p17).

The lack of affective physical affirmation has been linked to the following:

- Physical, social, emotional and cognitive deficits
- Memory loss and brain degeneration
- Suicidal ideation and self-destructive behaviours (such as self-harm, eating disorders, alcoholism and substance abuse)
- Difficulties in experiencing love coupled with an extraordinary need for it
- Increased vulnerability to stress
- Poor inhibitory control and lack of self-soothing abilities
- Depression, anxiety and a deep sense of alienation and isolation
- Inability to develop affectionate bonds and feel any emotions deeply
- An aversion to being touched
- Lack of trust and fear of intimacy
- Higher susceptibility to illness
- Sexual dysfunction
- Lower life expectancy and in extreme cases infant death.

Conversely, a substantial interdisciplinary body of research shows that a comforting touch does the following:

- Supports cognitive development and improves learning
- Increases self-worth, resilience and creativity
- Fosters positive body image

- Facilitates impulse control
- Lowers blood pressure and heart rates
- Eases symptoms of anxiety and depression
- Fosters feelings of trust and contentment
- Promotes social bonds and improves our abilities to be sensitive to the needs of others
- Strengthens the immune system
- Stimulates the release of endorphins, the body's natural pain suppressors
- Increases weight gain and faster growth in premature babies.

(Davis, 1999; Keltner, 2009; Hess, 2014)

Touch and adolescent development

There's no doubt that we are tactile beings and our need for affectionate physical intimacy remains a necessity throughout our lives. Not only is it essential to our physical and psychological health, it is also central to human communication and is our richest means of emotional expression (Keltner, 2009). Touch is the universal language of love and attachment. Empirical evidence even suggests that tactile stimulation is a considerably more accurate way to convey relational messages and decode emotions than verbal communication or facial expressions (Hertenstein, 2006). Yet communication experts and developmental psychologists report that by the time children reach adolescence, they receive only half as much daily positive touching as they did in the early part of their lives (Field, 2001). Considering the importance of touch on social and emotional growth, and since one of the central tasks of adolescence is the maturation of interpersonal skills necessary for adult relationships, the need for physical affection is as critical during this transitional stage of development as it is during childhood. In fact, researchers at the University of Miami Touch Research Institute found that adolescents who experience significant daily amount of positive physical intimacy, such as kissing, stroking and hugging, exhibit far less depression symptoms and aggressive behaviour than those who have minimal physical affection with their caregivers.

Although research findings amply demonstrate the link between juvenile delinquency, emotional disturbances and the frequency of positive touch, our interventions are rarely complemented by a positive physical contact experience (Field, 1999, 2002). Our children are growing in a world of physical, emotional and social disconnection and are at risk of turning into touch-avoidant adults. Mass media reports of child molestation, coupled with our fears that touch might be interpreted as sexually motivated, has resulted in strict 'hands-off' policies and restrictive hugging regulations for many organisations working with young people. However, declaring a prohibition on hugging and other displays of affection is likely to intensify young people's cravings for touch and drive them to satisfy their 'skin hunger' through violent encounters or promiscuity. Negative touching (even the kind that brings physical or emotional pain) is better than no touch at all. As Montagu states, many adolescents who engage in sexual activities prematurely are often seeking closeness and cuddling from another human being rather than sexual pleasure. They '*use their newly acquired genital capacity and coitus to meet the need for touching, for being held*' (1971, p211).

The holding environment

Touch is as essential to our survival and growth as food and water. In the words of the renowned American family therapist Virginia Satir, '*We need four hugs a day for survival. We need eight hugs a day for maintenance. We need twelve hugs a day for growth*'.[28]

Although touch within a safe and trusting environment can contribute significantly to the recovery of individuals who suffered adverse childhood experiences, it is not always possible or wise to physically hug an adolescent

---

[28] Research shows that to optimize the flow of both the 'love hormone' oxytocin and the 'happiness hormone' serotonin, not only does it need to be a frontal heart-to-heart hug, but the embrace must be held for at least six seconds (Rubin, 2009).

as it may trigger negative interpretations rooted in past trauma, particularly for survivors of sexual abuse (Cerio, 2004). However the physical holding can be replicated through symbolic containment in a nurturing relational space in which the adolescent feels emotionally held.

The concept of the 'holding environment' (Winnicott, 1965) is modelled on the protective holding of an infant and the mutuality of experience between a nurturing and responsive caregiver and her child. It implies feelings of physical and emotional safety without confinement (Benjamin, 1998). A study done in 2000, published by the Committee on Integrating the Science of Early Childhood Development, confirms that healthy child development relies heavily on the role of the mother as a container for the infant's anxieties and on the non-verbal emotional exchanges that take place between them (Shonkof *et al*, 2000). When the infant experiences an intolerable anxiety, he deals with it by projecting it into the mother. This allows him to both evacuate and communicate what is internally unbearable. If in return he feels affectionately held and perceives his mother as a responsive and empathic other capable of bringing relief, he will then reabsorb what was initially intolerable in a more manageable form. In the process, he will also internalise the containing function of his mother and gradually develop his own ability to hold and soothe himself (Segal, 1975). Conversely if the mother is unable to serve as a positive model for containing powerful negative states, the original anxiety is returned in unmodified form, and the infant's ability for affective self-regulation is at risk. For, as Gerhardt states, '*It is impossible to generate the attitude of self-care and awareness of one's own feelings if someone else hasn't first done it to you*' (2004, p110).

Therefore if we see behaviour as communication, the aggression displayed by emotionally wounded adolescents could be understood as a deep yearning for environmental stability, a furious and desperate attempt to coerce others to provide them with the holding they so sorely missed in their early years. Or, in the words of Winnicott, '*The urge to get back behind the moment of deprivation and so to undo the fear of the unthinkable anxiety'* (1967, p92). To put it another way, these lawless and disrespectful young people are searching for holding because they lack the strength and capacity to hold themselves together (Pestalozzi, 1999). Their destructive behaviour is a sign that they have not abandoned all hopes of having their infantile needs met by a caring and sensitive other. Thus our primary task is to provide them with a safe, compassionate, predictable and robust environment so that they may have the opportunity to resume an emotional development that had become stalled and they may gradually develop their own internal holding system. In short, in order to put psychological development back on track we need to go back with them to the moment of deprivation and provide them with a reparative emotional experience akin to re-parenting. The following reminders serve as a template for the development of such relational space in which powerful affects can be safely expressed, contained and processed.

Be attentive to the flow of experiencing going on within ourselves, and learn to be both robust and vulnerable

Just as we need to be open to our suffering before we can open ourselves to the suffering of others, we ought to be attentive to the flow of experiencing going on within ourselves before we can help adolescents become aware of theirs. It is also important to remember that the powerful feelings they often trigger in us are not only connected to what they cannot hold in themselves but might be linked to our own attachment history. Therefore we must be aware of our personal blocks so that no inner barriers can prevent us from entering fully into a genuine relationship based on mutual trust and respect. Our ability to untangle what belongs to the adolescent and what belongs to us, as well as our capacity to contain and manage both our anxieties and those of the adolescent, is of critical importance. It allows us to communicate that powerful emotional states can be deeply felt and survived rather than acted out. See chapters 3 and 4.

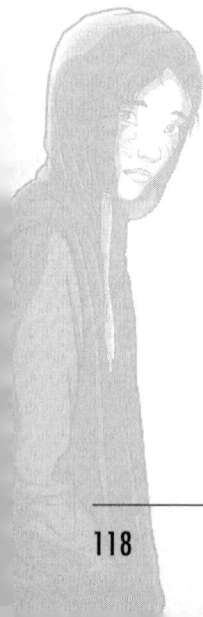

Speechmark

Welcome all emotions with equal warmth, and hold for adolescents what they cannot carry for themselves

Our willingness to hold for adolescents what they cannot yet carry for themselves (ie contain their projections) and act as an empathic mirror in which they can safely explore their unwanted feelings and meet their neglected developmental needs will in turn increase their ability to self-regulate and respond to situations creatively and flexibly. For, as Fonagy notes, '*the psychological self develops through perception of oneself in another person's mind as thinking and feeling*' (2001, p167). See chapter 6.

Provide empathy

In echoing Kohut (1984), Khan insists that when working with individuals who have suffered empathic failure in childhood, we must let go of our preconceptions and be willing to learn with them and from them. Our role is to adopt a not-knowing and curious stance, strive for the deepest possible understanding of their reality and sensitively share with them the emotional impact their affects have on us. This implies we need to open ourselves to the empathic experience that will allow us to see the world from their perspectives. To put it another way, we must emotionally and imaginatively enter into their subjective worlds and experience their reality as fully as possible while remaining in touch with our own internal process and individuality. This empathic understanding is the essential element that allows adolescents to stay connected with anxiety-provoking materials and tolerate painful affects without fragmenting or acting out and with time enables them to develop their capacities to regulate and modulate powerful affective states. See chapter 4.

Use symbolic communication and the creative media

The expressive arts, together with the facilitation of a safe and reliable environment, promote self-actualisation and facilitate impulse control.

They enable adolescents to both communicate and to contain otherwise overwhelming thoughts and emotions (Carey, 2006). We will discuss this important concept in more detail in chapter 17.

Adopt a non-defensive stance, and work on understanding rather than reacting

Our willingness to form a safe and secure holding environment is conveyed implicitly and explicitly through our tolerance, patience, unconditional acceptance and our ability to respond in non-disruptive and non-retaliatory ways to threats or efforts at manipulation (Langs, 1976). In other words, when we find ourselves under attack the first rule is not to fight back (Khan, 2001). The negative feelings adolescents direct towards us shouldn't be met with a defensive countermove. Instead we must aim to adopt an attitude of acceptance and curiosity as to where they originate from and be open to the possibility that we might have (consciously or unconsciously) contributed to the situation. See chapters 3 and 4.

Be playful

It is through early play that children learn about the world and how to navigate their environments. It increases their capacities to work cooperatively with others, facilitates problem-solving abilities and allows them to imagine and try out new possibilities without being directly at risk. Not only is imaginative play and make-believe critical for early social, emotional and creative development, but it remains a key to growth and creativity throughout life. And it is only by being creative that the individual unlocks his potential and discovers his own unique and autonomous self (Winnicott, 1971). As Dr Stuart Brown, the founder of the National Institute for Play, remarks, 'Play is called recreation because it makes us new again, it re-creates us and our world' (2010, p127). See chapter 8.

Stay in the here-and-now

Finally, it is best to focus on what is happening, the moment-to-moment process, rather than on the adolescent's history. A direct reactivation of past traumatic memories is likely to abruptly reawaken anxiety-provoking material and elicit a protective aggressive response. Conversely, our ability to be present in the moment and focus on the here-and-now, rather than the there-and-then, lessens the risk of damage occurring to the alliance. This does not mean we ignore his previous experiences but that we focus on the impact the past has on the present. The rationale behind that approach rests upon the understanding that shame-based memories and unresolved infantile anxieties remain active within the personal unconscious and constantly impact upon his present interactions. In short, the young person's relational difficulties originate from painful attachment experiences, and these past interpersonal problems will progressively emerge in the here-and-now of the relationship where they can then be contained and safely explored (Yalom, 2002). See chapter 2.

A warning

A consistent holding environment provides both a secure container and a buffer for surges of unprocessed shame-based affects. It promotes growth, fosters behavioural changes and allows for experiences of closeness and autonomy (Basham & Miehls, 2004). Yet we ought to acknowledge that adolescents whose sense of trust and safety have been shattered, will inevitably need to test our abilities to hold the boundaries of such space. Thus when challenged, we aim to resist the impulse to force our wills upon them but hold on to the thought that their disruptive behaviour serves to assess how reliable their environment is. We strive to remain empathically present, promote their active participation in the problem-solving process and demonstrate our capacity to respond flexibly and creatively to external stimuli and internal states. For the way we influence others most deeply is by example (Hendrix, 1991).

Conclusion

Although both inappropriate childhood touching experiences and the lack of physical affirmation can force individuals to forsake their relational needs and seek refuge in compensatory worlds of fantasy, empathic holding provides adolescents with opportunities to repair their relationships with reality and create new and healthier patterns of relating. Therefore we must aim to create an alliance based on hope, trust, love, autonomy, patience, respect and non-defensiveness and strive to be both vulnerable enough to invite a meaningful relationship and robust enough to maintain the boundaries of the holding space. This is, without a doubt, a slow and laborious task. The capacity for trust has its origins in early mother-child experiences. Our earliest interactions create relational patterns and attachment schemas that inform our subsequent relationships. Thus adolescents who were deprived of empathic attunement or maternal care are highly unlikely to let us get close to them, let alone welcome our offers for support with wide-open arms. But a compassionate approach, coupled with a reflective and open attitude, and a recognition of their need not to trust, may in time reduce their defensive responses (Meissner, 1996). As the following case study highlights, new and corrective emotional experiences need to be consistent and frequent until they are fully integrated (Taransaud, 2011).

REFERENCES

Basham K & Mielhls D (2004) *Transforming the Legacy*, Columbia University Press, New York.

Benjamin J (1998) *The Bonds of Love: Psychoanalysis, Feminism, and the Problem of Domination*, Pantheon Books, New York.

Bjornsdotter M, Gordon I, Pelphrey KA, Olausson H, Kaiser MD (2014) 'Development of brain mechanisms for processing affective touch'. Published in *Frontiers in Behavioural Neuroscience*, 8, p24. US National Library of Medicine.

Breuning L (2011) *I, Mamals, Why Your Brain Links Status and Happiness*, Inner Mammal Institute, Oakland, CA.

Speechmark

Brown S (2010) *Play: How It Shapes the Brain, Opens the Imagination, and Invigorates the Soul*, Penguin Books, New York.

Carey L (2006) *Expressive and Creative Arts Methods for Trauma Survivors*, Jessica Kingsley, London.

Cerio D (2004) 'Touch, the unspoken language: healing from sexual abuse', published in *Skinship Magazine,* 1(2).

Davis P (1999) *The Power of Touch: The Basis for Survival, Health, Intimacy, and Emotional Well-Being*, Hay House, Carlsbad, CA.

Field T (1999) 'American adolescents touch each other less and are more aggressive toward their peers as compared with French adolescents', Published in *Adolescence*, 34, pp753–8. Maryland: US National Library of Medicine.

Field T (2001) *Touch*, MIT Press, Cambridge, MA.

Field T (2002) 'Violence and touch deprivation in adolescents', published in *Adolescence*, 37, pp753–8. US National Library of Medicine, Maryland.

Fonagy P (2001) *Attachment Theory and Psychoanalysis*, Other Press, New York.

Fortuna K & Knafo A (2014) 'Parental and genetic contributions to prosocial behaviour', Padilla-Walker L and Carlo G (eds), *Prosocial Development: A Multidimensional Approach*, Oxford University Press, Oxford.

Frazer A & Hensler J (1999) 'Serotonin', Siegel J, Agranoff BW, Albers RW, Fisher SK & Uhler MD (eds), *Basic Neurochemistry, Molecular, Cellular, and Medical Aspects*, 6th edn, Lippincott Williams & Wilkins, Philadelphia, PA.

Gerhardt S (2004) *Why Love Matters: How Affection Shapes a Baby's Brain*, Brunner-Routledge, East Sussex.

Hendrix H (1991) 'Creating the false self', Zweig C (ed) *Meeting the Shadow: The Hidden Power of the Dark Side of Human Nature*, Penguin, New York.

Hertenstein M (2006) 'Touch communicates distinct emotions', *Emotion*, 6 (3), pp528–33. Washington: The American Psychological Association.

Hess S (2014) *Touch: The Power of Human Connection*, Fulcrum Solutions, Oregon.

Howe, D (2005) *Child Abuse and Neglect: Attachment, Development, and Intervention*, Palgrave Macmillan, Hampshire.

Keltner D (2009) Born to Be Good: *The Science of a Meaningful Life*, W. W. Norton, New York.

Khan M (2001) *Between Therapist and Client, The New Relationship* (rev edn), Holt Paperbacks, New York.

Kohut H (1984) *How Does Analysis Cure?*, The University of Chicago Press, Chicago, IL.

Langs R (1976) *The Therapeutic Interaction* (Vols 1 & 2), Jason Aronson, New York.

Malone D (2013) *Metamorphosis and the Science of Change*, BBC4 documentary, London.

Meissner WW (1996) *The Therapeutic Alliance*, Yale University Press, New Haven, CT.

Michaels J (2010) *The Today Show: Morning News TV Program*, National Broadcasting Company (NBC), New York.

Montagu A (1971) *Touching: The Significance of the Skin*, Harper & Row, New York.

Passamonti L (2011) 'Voice of reason needs serotonin', published in *New Scientist*, 2831; September 2011.

Pestalozzi J (1999) 'Containment and the body of the analyst: on psychotic transference in adolescence', Anastasopoulos D, Laylou-Lignos E & Waddell M (eds), *Psychoanalytic Psychotherapy of the Severely Disturbed Adolescent*, Karnac Books, London.

Rubin G (2009) *The Happiness Project: Or Why I Spent a Year Trying to Sing in the Morning, Clean My Closets, Fight Right, Read Aristotle, and Generally Have More Fun*, Harper Collins, New York.

Segal H (1986) A Psychoanalytic Approach to the Treatment of Schizophrenia (1975). In *The Work of Hanna Segal: A Kleinian Approach to Clinical Practice*, Free Association Books, London.

Shonkoff J, Phillips DA & National Research Council (US) (2000) *From Neurons to Neighborhoods: The Science of Early Childhood Development: The Science of Early Childhood Development*, The National Academy Press, Washington, DC.

Taransaud D (2011) *You Think I'm Evil: Practical Strategies for Working with Aggressive and Challenging Adolescents*, Worth Publishing, London.

Winnicott D (1990) Delinquency as a Sign of Hope; a talk given to the Assistant Governors' Conference, held at King Alfred's College, Winchester, April 1967, published in *Home is Where we Start From*, Penguin Books, London (first published in 1986).

Winnicott DW (1990) *The Maturational Processes and the Facilitating Environment*, Karnac Books, London (first published in 1965).

Winnicott DW (2005) *Playing and Reality*, Routledge Classics, Oxon. First published in 1971.

Yalom I (2002) *The Gift of Therapy: Reflections on Being a Therapist*, Piatkus Books, London.

15

DANNI AND THE STALKER; LOVED TO DEATH

It hurts. Not just in the imagination. Not just in the mind. It's a soul-hurt.
A body hurt. A real gets-inside-you-and-rips-you-apart pain. I hate love.

Neil Gaiman
(*The Sandman*, vol. 9. 1996, p219)

Danni was a 13-year-old adolescent who, from infancy to age four, had been violently abused by her drug addict mother and her revolving door of boyfriends. Danni and I had been working together for over three years, and both her capacity for awareness and intimacy had considerably increased. Our work was coming to a natural end and we were reflecting and reminiscing on the journey we took together.

Danni: *To tell you the truth, at the beginning I wasn't too keen on you.*

The feelings were mutual. At the start I was not too keen on her either. For the first two years our sessions were fraught with many manipulative attempts to control my behaviour and sabotage any hope for genuine intimacy. Although Danni rarely missed a session, she relentlessly challenged my professional competence. She arrived late and left early, intimidated other students, made outrageous demands, stole resources and regularly threatened to frame me with false sexual accusations. But over time, and with many failures and setbacks, our relationship gradually developed and grew into a robust working alliance of mutual trust and respect. Danni now felt sufficiently secure to calmly voice negative feelings she had towards me and to know that I would not be burdened by her disclosure and that her revelation would not damage our relationship.

Me:	*I really appreciate your honesty. What was it about me that you were not too keen on?*

Danni:	*To tell you the truth,* she repeated, *I thought you were a stalker.*

Her words sent a shiver down my spine. I wondered what her definition of a stalker was.

Danni:	*The closer a stalker is, the more dangerous he gets. A stalker is someone who loves to death.*

With a few simple words Danni had summed up both our early interactions and her past experiences of love and intimacy.

Reflection

Traumatic early experiences, accompanied by a lack of reparation from the caregiver, leave deep imprints on the developing brain. Negative relational templates set down early in life, and hardened through repeated confirmatory life experiences, disrupt the healthy growth of relational neuronal pathways. This can result in biased information processing, distorted world views and hypervigilant behaviour against real and imagined threats in subsequent relationships.

Children rely on their primary caregivers to help them make sense of the world and define themselves and others. But when that first love brings pain and rejection, the whole world turns into a dangerous place where intimacy goes hand in hand with abuse. If the giver of life is also the source of terror, the part of the brain involved in associative fear memory is etched with the message that love equates hurt. Whenever new stressors resemble those previously endured, painful affects resurface and give rise to violent manipulative strategies designed to protect from further hurt and humiliation.

So, in view of Danni's past, her defensive actions made perfect sense. What she dreaded most in our relationship was the reliving of painful childhood

Speechmark Ⓢ

experiences, and violence was the only way she could manage her fear of closeness and vulnerability. For, as Richo (1997) notes, when we ask someone who is afraid of our love to let us get close, what we are really asking her to do is to 'die of fright'. The horrific abuse Danni suffered at the hands of the people she once depended upon kept her stuck in a state of permanent arousal and on high alert for anything threatening in her surroundings. Every attempt at forming a secure holding environment was read through the template of earlier relationships and triggered an internal alarm that was promptly followed by a protective aggressive response. So Danni perceived me as a stalker, a predator who, in the name of love, instils fear in his victims and restricts their movements until they are no longer in control of their lives. Or, as she gravely put it: *someone who loves to death.*

Me: *It makes complete sense. You had very good reasons to think I was a stalker. But now we trust each other. You have allowed me to get very close to your hurt. Help me understand what changed?*

Danni: *What changed? Nothing changed. Every time I came here, no matter what I did, no matter what I said, you carried on caring for me, and that scared me. I thought you were a stalker. But after two years you still cared for me. Nothing changed. So I thought you were safe.*

Conclusion

Building a strong and robust alliance with an adolescent whose sense of safety has been shattered is a long and arduous process that requires not only empathic fortitude, resilience and emotional robustness but also determination verging on tenacity.[29] And although moving beyond the resistance is important for those whose early development was distorted by

---

[29] Possibly one of the most powerful descriptions of a sense of trust shattered by abuse and betrayal comes from Mollon (1996). He compares the experience to a gang of Hell's Angels breaking into a church and rapping the congregation: something smashes into a sacred space.

---

terror and coercive control, resisting contact is equally important, in that the adolescent asserts herself and does not accommodate to our needs (Wieland, 1998). Thus, considering the impact of trauma on the security of attachment and emotional functioning, adolescents will need to test their environments and challenge our abilities to maintain a consistent and assertive stance in setting limits. They will also need the freedom to move at their own pace, and not at the pace which we feel they should. They have structured their world in such a way that their relational capacities and vulnerability remain hidden and unacknowledged. To limit contact and shield the shamed wounded self of their childhood, they have erected a solid, impenetrable wall between them and the world. A wall they began building early in life, until it reached such height that it became impossible for them to see what was on the other side. And if they cannot see the other side, neither can they be aware of the wall (Philipson, 2001). Our role is not to brashly challenge their perceptions or tear down the protective structures they have built around their hurt but to help them readjust their defences so that they are high enough to provide sufficient protection against injury yet low enough to allow sufficient contact with their environment. This is a slow process that is more likely to succeed through learning-by-imitation than direct teaching or lecturing. Indeed, it is highly improbable that adolescents will willingly reassess the strategies they have learned through years of self-preservation just because we ask them to. But since our most valuable resource is our own self and the way we influence children most deeply is by example, initially it is our own behaviour that will serve best as a model for our young people's coping behaviour (Hendrix, 1991; Frydenberg, 1997). Thus, it is by containing both their anxieties and ours, and living as an example of tolerance, patience, understanding and non-defensiveness, that we will convey the message that robustness and vulnerability can coexist and that they can only be understood in relation to one another (Etkin, 2016). And with time, we can hope, help them repair their relationships with reality and discover that lowering their defences will not render them helpless.

REFERENCES

Etkin D (2016) *Disaster Theory: An Interdisciplinary Approach to Concepts and Causes*, Butterworth-Heinemann, Oxford.

Frydenberg E (1997) *Adolescent Coping: Theoretical and Research Perspectives*, Routledge, London.

Gaiman N (1996) *The Sandman, Vol. 9: The Kindly Ones*, Vertigo, New York.

Hendrix H (1991) *Creating the False Self*, published in Meeting the Shadow: The Hidden Power of the Dark Side of Human Nature, Penguin, New York.

Mollon P (1996) *Multiples Selves, Multiple Voices: Working with Trauma, Violation and Dissociation*, Wiley, West Sussex.

Philipson P (2001) *Self in Relation*, The Gestalt Journal Press, New York.

Richo D (1997) *When Love Meets Fear: How to Become Defense-less and Resource-full*, Paulist Press, Mahwah, NJ.

Wieland S (1998) *Techniques and Issues in Abuse-Focused Therapy with Children and Adolescents: Addressing the Internal Trauma*, Sage Publications, Thousand Oaks, CA.

16

OPERATING ON THE HUMAN HEART
(THE STICKY NOTE STRATEGY)

*If I feel nothing [...] I will be untouchable. I will be unscathed.
I will be invincible. I will be invisible. A ghost among the
wreckage of lives seeing everything and feeling nothing.*

Kathy Magliato
(*Heart Matters*, 2010, p208)

Operating on the human heart requires a degree of detachment and
imperturbability. Selzer remarks: '*The surgeon cannot weep. When he cuts
the flesh, his own must not bleed*' (1976, p101), but emotional detachment is
a double-edged sword. In her memoir, Dr Kathy Magliato, an internationally
renowned cardiothoracic surgeon, reveals how she used to be emotionally
and physically impervious to both her pain and that of her patients. She
writes: '*My heart was hard. I had this shield, this full metal jacket, and I
strapped that thing on every day and I went to work [...] it was the only thing
holding me together*' (2010, p56). During her first year of residency training,
she spent six months on the paediatric service operating on children with
congenital heart disease. She found herself caring for an 11-day-old baby
who was born with a large hole in her heart. The label on the incubator
simply read 'Baby Girl'. The child's parents, fearing their newborn would
not survive, did not name her. Following the surgery to close the hole in her
heart, Dr Magliato stayed at this little girl's bedside for 11 straight days.
Although she knew there was no way this child was going to make it, she
never left the hospital. In an interview with Janet Choi (2012) she discloses,
'*The whole eleven days I had been taking care of that baby I never touched
that baby. I never connected. Why would I? I had that full metal jacket on,
my job was just to keep that baby alive, I wasn't to touch that baby or be
connected with that baby in any way. I had that hard heart you know*'. On

the 11th day, the newborn was taken off life support. She died without a name and without her parents present. The nurses took the baby out of the incubator and let Kathy hold her for the first time. She reveals: *'The pain was unbearable, I could hardly look at her there in my arms as I fought back tears [...] But right then and there I made a choice. A choice that forever changed me. I chose to feel it all. I chose to find dignity, compassion, and kindness in this sweet child's death'* (2010, p208). After 'Baby Girl' took her last breath in Kathy's arms, she walked down the hallway to the parents' room while carrying their dead child. She kissed her on the forehead and handed her to her grieving mother who couldn't be there when she died. At that moment, Kathy says, *'I realised that I could take off that jacket, that I could connect with a patient, and that I wouldn't break in two'*.

Although detachment is written into the job description of the surgeon (Fisher, 1993), a considerable body of research shows that the stronger the bond between physician and patient, the better and faster the healing process occurs, for it is through compassion that suffering is released and transformed (Hamilton, 2013). Similarly, our work with emotionally wounded adolescents requires us to remove our full metal jacket. Only when we no longer shield ourselves from vulnerability can we allow ourselves to be moved by the fragility and suffering of others and see the world from their perspectives.

Empathy, the healing agent

Empathy is an integral part of the trust-building process. It is at the core of our interconnectedness and is key to building a safe and secure holding environment. It is the healing agent. The first step towards cultivating an empathic approach is to consider others as equal to ourselves while accepting that their realities might be different from ours. Rogers explains, *'it means entering the private perceptual world of the other and becoming thoroughly at home in it [...] It means temporarily living in the others life, moving about in it delicately without making judgments'* (1980, p142). He adds it also implies *'communicating [our] sensing of the person's world as [we] look with fresh unfrightened eyes at elements of which he or she is fearful'* (1980, p142).[30] So in order to help adolescents develop healthier relational patterns we need to enter into a wholehearted engagement with them and put ourselves in their internal worlds of perception. We also need to communicate our understanding for their experiences in a language attuned to those current feelings (Rogers *et al*, 1967). This means we need to experience their helplessness, powerlessness and their rage as if they were our own, but without our own helplessness, powerlessness or rage taking over us. Then we need to let them know that, given their personal histories, those feelings are understandable and normal responses (Khan, 2001).

But feeling at home with another requires vulnerability. It means feeling emotions we do not always want to feel. It means ceding control (Watcher-Boettcher, 2013). The following case study illustrates the difficulties of allowing ourselves to be vulnerably seen while on the receiving end of challenging behaviour. It also highlights the crucial importance of honest communication and emphasises that empathy has more to do with emotional knowing of another human being than intellectual understanding (Moore & Fine, 1967). Finally, it provides a simple yet effective strategy to help us stay grounded and provide adolescents with responses healthier than the ones they are accustomed to.

The sticky note strategy

During my childhood and early adolescence, 'flights into fantasy' allowed me to compensate for feelings of helplessness and inadequacy. By the time

---

[30] Perhaps one of the most beautiful definitions of empathic listening I have come across is in Carl Rogers's book *A Way of Being*. He compares the experience of being truly heard and understood to that of *'a prisoner in a dungeon tapping out day after day a Morse code message, "Does anybody hear me? Is anybody here?" And finally one day he hears some faint tappings which spell out "Yes". By that one simple response he is released from his loneliness; he has become human again'* (1980, p10).

I reached my mid-twenties, it was through intellectualisation that I had learned to distance myself from stressful situations. Strategic reasoning was my default coping mechanism, and although 'flights into reason' allowed me to bring painful affects under control, it negatively impacted upon my ability to build meaningful relationships with others, particularly with my clients. Every time I came face to face with an adolescent who reawakened old wounds, triggered my insecurities or made me feel emotions I did not want to feel, rather than explore the here-and-now of the experience and focus on building a heartfelt relationship, I immediately sought refuge in emotional detachment. I intellectualised and threw logic at my inner monsters.

In my second year of training I was offered a placement in a centre for adolescents with social, emotional and behavioural difficulties. Jon was my very first client. He was born with a large birthmark under his right eye and claimed that his father, a petty criminal and violent alcoholic, had punched him while he was in his mother's womb. And, as the popular saying goes, it was not a windy day when the apple fell from the tree. Jon was a troubled and troubling 13-year-old adolescent who had won the respect of his classmates through countless fights. Although he had no conviction as a juvenile, by the time he started secondary school, he had built quite a reputation for himself as the go-to guy for weed and pirated copies of the latest films and video games. He was barely two-thirds my height and half my age, yet I was intimidated by his complete disregard for the personal safety of himself and others. Each time I felt challenged by his behaviour, rather than use my immediate responses as instruments to guide my interventions and connect with the feelings behind his words and attitude, I intellectualised our encounters. I was aware of the disruptive feelings he triggered in me, but I refused to fully feel them. At best, I hid behind a mask of professional detachment and covered up my vulnerability behind canned responses and well-rehearsed communication techniques. Much like Weizenbaum's chatterbot 'Eliza'[31] (a conversational computer program that mimics a Rogerian psychotherapist), I used generic responses and reframed Jon's statements into questions. Like a recording machine on auto playback, I paraphrased, repeating verbatim without any empathy what he had said to me. At worse, I pushed my own agenda, gave out advice, evaluated his attitude from my own frame of reference and made assumptions based on superficial interpretations. Even when my lack of attunement resulted in me being the target of threats and ridicule, I valued cognitive reasoning more than emotional authenticity and firmly remained in my head. My rational mind was both my shield and my sword. I clearly understood that intellectualisation was a defence mechanism linked to my personal history, a self-deceptive strategy I used to avoid anxiety-provoking affects. I was also consciously aware that beneath Jon's tough exterior was a tormented, frightened and needy child, but I could not lower my guard and let my more vulnerable feelings surface. My attention was focused on analysing, evaluating, judging and interpreting.

I sought support and guidance from a trusted colleague. In my naivety I had hoped she could teach me how to have an empathic and authentic presence. But empathy is caught, not taught (Gordon, 2009). It only develops through meaningful engagement with supportive and sensitive others. She pointed out that as far as defence mechanisms went, intellectualisation was one of the better one. After all, a theoretical interest in other people's emotional states is better than no interest at all. She added that the recognition of another's suffering was the first step towards developing a

---

[31] In 1966, Joseph Weizenbaum, a pioneer in computer science at the Massachusetts Institute of Technology, wrote a program called 'Eliza'. The interactive program, based on Carl Rogers's communication model, allowed a computer user to interact with a virtual therapist. In spite of its inability to handle complexity and nuances, many participants who conversed with Eliza shared intimate details of their lives and believed the program understood their problems. Since then more advanced conversational character programs have been developed. In 2014, psychologist Albert Rizzo and computer scientist Louis-Philippe Morency created 'Ellie', a virtual therapist capable of reading and responding to human emotions. The avatar was designed to assess signs of depression and help veterans deal with PTSD.

more compassionate approach and said that with time I'd figure out a way to quieten the internal chatter in my brain so that I could connect with both Jon's vulnerability and mine.

I found little comfort in her words. I was too impatient. What I wanted was a practical solution, and I wanted it now. I had to find a way to be more authentic with Jon and myself. But how could I give up control and experiment with new ways of being? How could I connect with Jon's vulnerability and be more in sync with mine? Simple, I would coerce my mind to think differently.

Every time I need to remember something important I use strategic triggers such as sticky notes to remind me of what I have to do. So I thought I'd employ a similar strategy. I stuck a few sticky notes on the walls in my room and wrote the letters B.R (Be Real) on every single one. I then gave myself a little pep talk, for, as neuroscientist Jill Bolte-Taylor (2009) remarks, self-talks can help focus the mind and allow for new patterns of thinking and behaviour to take root. So I told myself that every time I'd see a sticky note I'd relax into the moment, slow down long enough to experience the feelings aroused within me and use them as data to guide my interventions. I somehow hoped that, like an actor who through repetition masters the emotions that animate his character and becomes one with the part he is to play, this strategy would support my practice.

Confident that this fail-proof plan was going to solve all my problems and help me keep both my head and heart in the game, I patted myself on the back and waited for Jon. But things did not go exactly the way I had planned. I had failed to consider two important factors: Jon's ability at detecting incongruities and his keen sense of observation. As he walked into the room, Jon immediately noticed the sticky notes. He walked straight past me with a slow swagger that gave of a 'I'm a bad boy' vibe, removed the notes from the wall, looked at me with a blank stare and asked, '*What is that for?*' I was not prepared for that. I felt a rush of blood to my head. My cheeks were burning.

I felt exposed. But I forced myself to remain calm. I paused. I took stock of my feelings, and for the first time, instead of responding with defensive manoeuvres, I took a chance. I allowed myself to be vulnerably seen.

> Me: *Well … uh … sometimes when we are together I think you try to tell me you're not happy with the way things are, but you tell me not in words, and sometimes I don't get it … so the sticky notes are there to remind me that I need to be more attentive to how you communicate and to what you say. 'Cause you deserve my full attention. And from now, when I do not understand you I won't pretend I do, instead I'll ask for your help.*

I thought I got away with it, but, like most adolescents who have endured adverse childhood experiences, Jon was acutely adept at reading non-verbal cues (Sanderson, 2010). He raised his chin and tilted his head to one side as if he were saying, '*I know there's more to it than that*'. I swallowed hard and took another deep breath.

> Me: *Uh … and sometimes when we are together, sometimes I feel really helpless … and sometimes I even feel scared … I don't always know where those big feelings come from, but when I feel them, I push them away. Rather than being honest with you and tell you how I'm feeling, I hide. I pretend I'm okay.*

Jon remained still. His arms folded across his chest, and his face betrayed no emotions. He just kept staring at me.

> Me: *So these sticky notes are also there to remind me that I need to acknowledge my feelings and be more real. Because if I can't be completely honest with myself, how can I be honest with you. And I think you deserve the truth.*

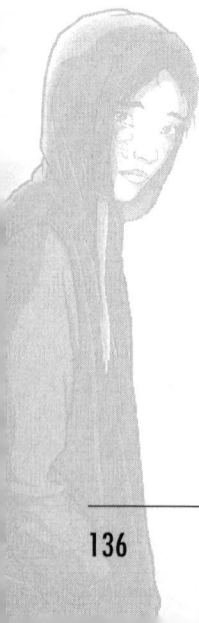

We stayed in silence for a few seconds

Me: *I guess that at times it must have felt like I wasn't really
        listening to you. You must have thought I was a fake …
        you must have thought I didn't care.*

Jon narrowed his eyes and nodded.

Me: *I'm sorry you experienced me as not caring … you had
        very good reasons to be angry with me … What is it like
        for you now to know that you have such an impact on
        me that sometimes I struggle to be genuine with you and
        don't give you my full attention?*

Jon remained still for a few seconds. He then put back the sticky notes on the
walls and said,

Jon: *That's cool!*

Although a theoretical understanding of trauma can help us better
comprehend the cause of aggressive behaviour, sometimes forming a
meaningful alliance has less to do with cognitive endeavours and more
to do with authenticity and a compassionate heart. Psychological growth
occurs only through genuine and intimate interactions with a caring other.
Miller and Stiver note that '*change occurs when the therapist can feel with a
person, that is, when the therapist can be moved emotionally by the person
and the person can be moved by the therapist*' (1997, p129). Although on
that particular day Jon did not appear to be impacted by my authenticity, the
effect my revelation had on our relationship was far deeper than I thought.
Two years after we stopped working together he paid me an unexpected visit.
As we were reminiscing, he said,

Jon: *You know, I always thought you were a good guy.*

Me: *Thank you, Jon, I'm touched.*

Jon: *No. Actually the first time I saw you I thought you'd never get me. But then you said 'Hi' and you gave me your hand to shake, so I thought I'd give you a chance.*

Most of the vulnerable young people we work with have never been welcomed into this world; greeting them with a smile and genuine warmth is crucial to the building of a meaningful relationship. Furthermore, the working alliance comes into play from the first moment of contact (Meissner, 1996), and as we discussed in chapter 14, not only touch fosters feelings of calm happiness and increases feelings of trust but it also floods our bodies with the bonding hormone oxytocin.

Jon then asked me if I remembered the day I had stuck sticky notes on my walls.

Me: *I remember that day very clearly. What was it like for you?*

Jon: *Man! That was emotional! That's the day I decided to give you my trust.*

Conclusion

We all make mistakes, but what matters is not the commission of errors but what we chose to do with them (Yalom, 2002). We ought to be honest with ourselves and with the young people in our care. As Khan (2001) notes, out of all the types of self-disclosure, acknowledging our failures helps others develop trust in us. So rather than cover up our shortcomings and display a false image of competency, we need to own up to our errors and bias. And sometimes we also need to say '*I am sorry*', for this allows us to model how to repair and rebuild relationships after a crisis, something most vulnerable young people have never experienced.

Being simultaneously robust and vulnerable when ridiculed or threatened is as much a matter of knowledge as of courage. And vulnerability is the

measurement of courage (Brown, 2012), and it is something we practice. The word 'courage' is derived from the Latin '*cor*', meaning heart. Brown explains, '*Courage originally meant to speak one's mind by telling all one's heart*' (2010, p12); it meant to speak honestly about our experiences and participate in the reality of another human being. Courage is risking vulnerability. It is presence and emotional flexibility. It is speaking from the heart and allowing our true self to be seen. As Dr Magliato discovered during her first year of residency training, to operate on the human heart, we need to remove our full metal jacket, adopt a non-defensive approach and find the strength to be comfortable with being uncomfortable, for discomfort is often a sign that new possibilities are emerging. Peck remarks, '*Our finest moments are most likely to occur when we are feeling deeply uncomfortable […] it is in such moments, propelled by our discomfort, that we are likely to step out of our ruts and start searching for different ways or truer answers*' (2003, p10).

As we have learned, although the ability to build a protective shell around our vulnerable self is one of our most valuable survival strategies, this suit of armour is not who we are, and it needs to be removed if we are to find compassion for ourselves and others (Alsford, 2006). In the following two chapters, we will explore approaches that will not only allow us to communicate our empathy and understanding to young persons but also open the path for more creative and healthier interactions between us and encourage them to share their stories.

REFERENCES

Alsford M (2006) *Heroes and Villains*, Darton, Longman & Todd, London.

Bolte-Taylor J (2009) *My Stroke of Insight*, Hodder & Stoughton, London.

Brown B (2010) *The Gifts of Imperfection*, Hazelden, Center City, MN.

Brown B (2012) *Listening to Shame*, TEDTalks, Houston, TX.

Choi J (2012) *How Love Affects Us Physically: A Heart Surgeon Weighs In*, OWN Channel, Chicago.

Fisher S & R (1993) *The Psychology of Adaptation to Absurdity: Tactics of Make Believe*, Psychology Press, Mahwah, NJ.

Gordon M (2009) *Roots of Empathy: Changing the World Child by Child*, Experiment Publishing, New York.

Hamilton F (2013) *Goodness to Go: A Handbook for Humanitarians*, First Edition Design Publishing, Sarasota, FL.

Khan M (2001) *Between Therapist and Client, The New Relationship* (revised edition), Holt Paperbacks, New York.

Magliato K (2010) *Heart Matters*, Three Rivers Press, New York.

Meissner WW (1996) *The Therapeutic Alliance*, Yale University Press, New Haven, CT.

Miller J & Stiver I (1997) *The Healing Connection*, Beacon Press, Boston, MA.

Moore B & Fine B (1967) *A Glossary of Psychoanalytic Terms and Concepts*, American Psychoanalytic Association, New York.

Rogers C (1980) *A Way of Being*, Houghton Mifflin Company, New York.

Rogers C, Stevens B, Gendlin ET, & Shlien JM (1994) *Person to Person: The Problem of Being Human*, Souvenir Press, London (first published in 1967).

Sanderson C (2010) *Introduction to Counselling Survivors of Interpersonal Trauma*, Jessica Kingsley, London.

Scott Peck M (2003) *Abounding Happiness: At Treasury of Wisdom*, Andrews McMeel Publishing, Kansas City, MO.

Selzer R (1996) *Mortal Lessons: Notes on the Art of Surgery*, Harcourt, New York (first published in 1976).

Watcher-Boettcher S (2013) The Pastry Box Project. 13th March 2013 (www.the-pastry-box-project.net/sara-wachter-boettcher/2013-march-18)

Yalom I (2002) *The Gift of Therapy: Reflections on Being a Therapist*, Piatkus Books, London.

AND A CHILD SHALL LEAD THEM

When you make it and paint it and perform it in painting it,
then you possess it, you make the monster your friend.

Joe Coleman

(Interview with Susanne Pfeffer for 'Internal Digging', 1997)

A pantheon of reviled mass murderers, cannibal killers, social outcasts and sideshow freaks populate the tormented paintings of Joe Coleman, a Brooklyn artist and collector of murderabilia. His works are archives of evening-news horror and human degradation in which nothing is off-limits. When describing Coleman's paintings, Shulins writes: '*Flesh rots. Sores weep. The flames of hell burn brightly. Perversion runs rampant. Things fall apart: Bodies. Cities. The whole social order*' (1997, p41). Coleman is essentially a storyteller. His pieces feature one central figure, upon whom the narrative is focused, with colourful vignettes and tiny cursives around them, which piece together both the ghastly deeds and the tragic lives of his subjects (Argento, 2003). Those portrayed include David Koresh, John Dillinger, Osama Bin Laden, Charles Manson and Joe himself. In a 2010 interview, he reveals, '*The subjects that I chose are the people who are disenfranchised, the losers. They don't get a chance to say their side of the story. So I'm going to give them their chance through me to say their side of the story. Not the cop side of the story. Not the forensic psychiatrist side of the story. Their side*' (Borowski, 2010).

Like Coleman's delicately crafted biographical paintings, our very Self is a collection of vignettes and internalised stories gathered from past encounters. These narratives, or life scripts, are an integral part of who we are; they shape our perceptions of the world and ourselves. They help us to structure experiences and organise self-concepts. But not only do stories contribute to the formation of identity, they also have a self-transforming role. They have the power to help us restructure our experiences, transform our perceptions and *'fold the worst events of life into a narrative of triumph'* (Solomon, 2014). As Turner and McIvor add, *'it is the working-through of the traumatic process that permits the development of a new story that is no longer about shame, humiliation, or guilt'* (1997, p213). Thus, it stands to reason that a crucial part of our work with emotionally wounded young people is to help them re-author their painful past experiences into a coherent narrative that can be explored and integrated into a life story. We must help them piece together a picture of their life history, reconnect with what has been repressed from conscious awareness and find a way to give a voice to their unspoken hurt. For, as Colfer remarks, *'a villain is just a victim whose story has not been told'* (2012, p9). A villain is a wounded soul who never had the opportunity to merge with the warmth and goodness of a caring other and share his story.

The child with bloodied knees

And a Child Shall Lead Them (2000) is an acrylic painting mounted on a 1960s schoolgirl's dress. It is the first piece in which Coleman used a child as his primary subject matter. The central figure is a sickly looking blue-eyed girl with bruised and bloodied knees. She exists in a world of cartoony atrocity that blurs the boundaries between innocence and brutality, a world where naughty girls squeeze little boys' necks and candies are amphetamines.

The child with bloodied knees is Mary Flora Bell, an 11-year-old girl who in 1968 killed two boys of four and three and was demonised across the country as a bad seed inherently evil and a child monster (Hari, 2009). Mary was born on Sunday 26 May 1957 at Dilston Hall Hospital in Gateshead to Betty Crikett, a 17-year-old single mother who later married Billy Bell, an alcoholic and lifelong criminal. Mary's birth was not greeted with joyful anticipation but with horror and rejection. *'Take the thing away from me'* were the first words her mother screamed when the nurse tried to place the newborn in her arms. Betty worked as prostitute and specialised in sadomasochism. In the

first four years of Mary's life, she repeatedly attempted to kill her unwanted daughter and make her death look accidental. Mary was frequently rushed to the hospital for near-overdose on iron tablets and Drinamyl. On one occasion, after she had her stomach pumped and regained consciousness, three-year-old Mary told the doctors, '*me mum gave me the Smarties*' (Sereny, 1972). Eventually Betty decided to make the best of the situation. When Mary turned four, she began to use her young daughter as a sexual prop in her sadomasochistic scenarios, forcing her to perform oral sex on her clients. After that, Betty would reward her daughter with a bag of chips. When Mary turned nine, she did not need her mother to pimp her anymore. She regularly gave herself away to strangers in exchange for candies and half a crown. That's why her knees are bloody and bruised, explains Joe Coleman: '*She was always on her knees*' (Petros, 2003). Mary was not only forced to service her mother's clients but she was also made to watch acts of sexual violence, such as corporal punishment and erotic asphyxiation. Years of unrelieved physical and psychological abuse contributed to the events that occurred on 25 May and 31 July 1968. A day before her 11th birthday Mary strangled to death four-year-old Martin Brown in a condemned house in the Scotswood area. Two months later she strangled three-year-old Brian Howe and mutilated his genitals.

In the weeks prior to her arrest, Mary purposely drew attention to herself. She broke into a nursery and left a note confessing to Martin Brown's killing, sketched pictures of the boy's dead body in her school exercise book, boasted in the playground she was a murderer, attacked other children and was seen laughing and rubbing her hands when the coffin was brought out of the Howe's house. Mary did not try to hide her crimes; she wanted to be caught. Her actions were both distress calls and forms of communication, wordless utterances of the cruelty and hurt she herself had suffered. As the officer in charge of the case, Chief Inspector Dobson, remarked: '*There was a terrible playfulness about it, a terrible gentleness if you like, and somehow the playfulness made it more, rather than less, terrifying*' (Pietras, 2013).

It was Mary's way to communicate what words could never convey. When she suffocated her little victims, she re-enacted acts of erotic asphyxiation she witnessed her mother inflicting on her clients as well as the terror she endured when they forced their penises into her mouth until she choked or passed out. As Mary painfully describes 28 years later, '*I had been picked up by my throat lots of times, by my mother, by some of the clients. When my mother used to pull my head back, with the throat stretched, she used to say, "it won't hurt ..." and then I'd lose consciousness and then wake up I'd hear her or them say, "it'll be alright ..."*' (Sereny, 1998, p345). She might have thought Martin Brown and Brian Howe would eventually wake up like she did after passing out. She did not understand the permanence of death: '*I strangled [them], but I thought of, you know, "play dead" [...] I must have been messed up inside*' (p87). Mary was caught on 5 August 1968 and convicted of manslaughter on the grounds of diminished responsibility on 17th December. After two years at the Red Bank secure unit (the same facility where Jon Venables would serve his sentence 25 years later), 13-year-old Mary wrote a letter to her mother in the form of a poem.

> *Please mam, put my tiny mind at ease,*
> *Tell judge and jury on your knees*
> *They will listen to your cry of pleas.*
> *The guilty one is you, not me.*
> *I sorry it has to be this way.*
> *We'll both cry and you will go away.*
> *Tell them you are guilty,*
> *Please, so then mam, I'll be free.*
> *(Sereny, 1998, p397)*

Coleman suggests that with guidance Mary might have become an artist, a poet or a writer (Wilson, 2012).

Joe Coleman has a rare understanding and a deep empathy with the villains and the outsiders that he paints. He often discloses that all his portraits are self-portraits and the process of art making is a way to create order out of inner chaos and transcend the darkness that otherwise might consume him. Like Mary, his childhood was tainted by fear and abuse. He was raised by a violent alcoholic war veteran and an ex–beauty queen excommunicated by the Catholic Church whose sexual energies were sometimes focused on him (Manley, 1998). In an Interview he reveals: '*That's why I have a certain amount of empathy for people whose lives took that direction but who as children, I feel, had similar feelings as I did. Their lives took a different path*' (Pfeffer, 1997).[32] Coleman sublimated his pain. Mary murdered. Had she been given the opportunity to safely express and process her hurt through the arts and in the presence of an empathic other, she might not have killed. For even though the diversion of destructive energies through sublimation does not automatically eliminate the source of the pain, it might have helped Mary channel her hurt towards less harmful outlets.

The healing Arts

To return to creative living, the fear networks associated with the traumatic episodes need to be reactivated so that unprocessed memories can be addressed, their meanings redefined and gradually integrated or assimilated into the survivor's autobiographical narrative (Van Vliet, 2010). The rationale behind this approach rests upon the understanding that pains and hurts cannot be reasoned away; as Khan puts it, the adolescent's '*difficulties were acquired through experience, they must be transformed through experience*' (2001, p57). But not only is the reliving of past painful memories likely to trigger a protective aggressive response, survivors are also limited in their ability to articulate their experiences. They do not have the words. Research and clinical observations confirm that unprocessed traumatic material presents itself in a dissociated form from autobiographic memory and

---

[32] It took Joe Coleman six-and-a-half month to complete *And a Child Shall Lead Them*, painting eight hours a day, concentrating one square inch at a time with brushes as fine as needles. After having lived over half a year in Mary Bell's world, he decided not to sell the painting. In Juxtapoz Magazine Coleman says: '*After I got married and started thinking about having kids, this painting was the kid that was produced*' (Petros, 2003). Mary became his symbolic offspring.

semantic access (Schauer, 2011). In other words, the emotional intensity of painful past experiences makes it difficult for survivors to piece together a coherent narrative of what happened. They can no longer tell their stories. So if traumatic memories are encoded as non-verbal memories, how can we help adolescents share their stories? We bypass language altogether.

The use of metaphors and symbolic imagery provide an indirect, non-threatening way of communicating deep and often painful thoughts and experiences that have defied verbal expression but continue to crave recognition (Robbins, 1980). Among the multitude of benefits a creative approach offers, some of which are particularly relevant to our work with adolescents.

The process of art making, together with the facilitation of a safe and reliable environment:

- provides a healthy distance from overwhelming affects associated with painful past experiences
- decreases behavioural problems and improves locus of control
- bypasses language and offers a deeper truth
- brings new insights and fosters self-renewal
- allows the survivor to move past trauma
- provides a safe and secure three-way relationship between the adolescent, the adult and the artwork
- builds a bridge between inner realms and outer experiences.

Provides a healthy distance from overwhelming affects associated with painful past experiences

When teaching poetry, Professor Wilson notes that if the poet is too close or too far from the scene he is describing, he'll lack clarity of vision, and he won't be able to clearly see the textures, contours, colours and how the various elements connect with their surroundings (2012). Therefore he will struggle to find the words to accurately express his thoughts and feelings.

Similarly the emotionally wounded adolescent needs the right psychological distance in order to confront anxiety-provoking material and articulate his thoughts and feelings rather than act them out or defend against them. The Arts provide the necessary psychological safety from which he can actively explore his painful past without fearing the full-blown reactivation of traumatic memories. Symbolic communication functions as a permeable buffer that permits safe access to past hurt but protects from feelings of shame and anxieties. It allows survivors to remain *'emotionally connected in the here and now in a safe relationship and setting while telling and re-experiencing their stories'* (Campbell, 2010, p202).

Decreases behavioural problems and improves locus of control

As discussed in chapters 1 and 2, when aggressive impulses are denied satisfactory outlets, they become more violent in nature and the individual's potential for creativity diminishes (Meadow, 2003). Conversely, when destructive urges press for expression and are channelled through artistic means, the individual develops his capacity to respond creatively and flexibly to ongoing life events rather than relying on outdated coping strategies, such as aggression, manipulation or withdrawal. Not only does the artwork function as a container for destructive thoughts and feelings, but the process of art making in the presence of an empathic witness lessens the likelihood of violence towards self and others. It enables the adolescent to tolerate and process intense emotional responses. The invitation to graphically express a powerful feeling instead of acting it out physically is a way of taming impulsive drive discharge and promoting healthy social functioning (Wilson, 2001).

Bypasses language and offers a deeper truth

Words frequently fail to convey the depth and complexity of intense emotional experiences. Furthermore, young people who have been subjected to severe shame, fear and humiliation in their early years are often unable to verbalise thoughts and feelings associated with the traumatic events. The creative media provides a powerful non-verbal form of communication to describe experiences that cannot be put into words. It goes beyond speechless terror and provides a unique and viable language to speak creatively about the unspeakable. It permits adolescents to safely externalise their hurt and shame without open acknowledgement of their own frightening experiences (Webb, 2006).

Brings new insights and fosters self-renewal

Creativity is a drive common to all beings that promotes self-actualisation and allows for new understandings to emerge (Moustakas, 1977). The Arts make the invisible visible. Creating visual metaphors of internal states provides a tangible record of inner experiences. What previously hid in the inner realm becomes part of the outer world where it can be seen and known. Once what was previously hidden or forgotten is 'out there', the adolescent, with the facilitation of a sensitive other, can safely explore and reconnect with emotions that were previously sealed off from conscious awareness. He is reacquainted with a piece of his lost history that can then be integrated into a larger self-concept. As the famous British psychoanalyst Donald Winnicott confirms, '*it is only in being creative that the individual discovers the self*' (1971, p73).

Allows the survivor to move past trauma

Early emotional wounding can leave a lasting imprint on the brain that keeps the victim trapped in the nightmare of the past (Goleman, 1996). Numerous neurobiological researches demonstrate that by giving shape to inexpressible thoughts and feelings, traumatic images can be unfrozen and altered, thus allowing the individual to safely confront, reorganise and process painful affects associated with past experiences, take a forward step towards change and with time and support move past the traumatic event (Anderson, 2001).

Provides a safe and secure three-way relationship between the adolescent, the adult and the artwork

The existence of the art product as a separate entity allows both the teen and adult to explore the young person's feelings and experiences more objectively. To assign powerful emotions to the play material or the image helps create a healthy distance from traumatic reminders while simultaneously reducing the distance between the adult and the adolescent as they form a relationship with each other by their mutual focus on a third thing, the artwork (Wieland, 1998; Taransaud, 2011). As Milia remarks in her book on violent creation, 'when aspects of the self are projected into the artwork rather than upon (the adult) there is less threat of damage occurring to the relationship' (2000, p182).

Builds a bridge between inner realms and outer experiences

The creative process puts an end to division. It creates a bridge between inner realms and outer realities, facts and fantasy, conscious and unconscious, the visible and the unseen. It links what previously appeared unconnected and brings conflicting forces into a common space where they can coexist and live side by side. Therefore the Arts provide an active platform where the interplay of polar opposites can be contained, tolerated and examined. They offer a fertile ground where the individual can organise his experiences of inner and outer worlds into a coherent form and integrate fragmented trauma memories and intrapsychic conflicts into a new narrative that promotes healing, enhances resilience and nurtures hope.

A warning: we do not possess superior vision

Although every work of art has a life of its own, separate from that of its maker (Kramer & Ulman 1992), and is therefore likely to trigger an emotional reaction within us, we must refrain from judgement and superficial interpretations or link their symbolic expressions to their personal history.

Indeed, adolescents often experience interpretations as attacks on a highly vulnerable, fragmented self (Pestalozzi, 1999). Instead we ought to stay with the 'not knowing'. We must let the image lead the way, respectfully engage the adolescent in a process of discovery, walk by his side and be willing to learn with him and from him. Our role is to create an *'ambience of supportive, but non intrusive contact'* (Kramer, 2001, p38), allow him to be in charge of the process, let the artwork become the focus of communication and only discuss feelings of worthlessness, shame, fear or despair in relation to the metaphor or creative exploration. By giving him the opportunity and the space to discover his own truth, we are empowering him to discover his own potential (Rogers, 2001).

Conclusion

The inability to verbalise their hurt and the fear of being overwhelmed by powerful emotions and losing control are the primary reasons why many traumatised young people appear resistant to directly discussing their painful past experiences (McNiff, 2001). Although cognitive and emotional avoidance is a common defensive mechanism that allows for normal functioning in the short term, it prevents the survivor from mastering painful affects and over time further maintains post-traumatic symptoms, such as aggression, social withdrawal, risk-taking behaviour, hypervigilance and exaggerated startle responses (Van der Kolk, 1996). Symbolic communication offers a non-verbal vehicle for the safe release of repressed emotions through metaphors and imagery. It provides a creative platform where adolescents can safely give a physical form to their pain, rage and fears, a space where they can confront traumatic reminders, tame the destructive energies associated with the experiences and rediscover that shame-based memories can be survived. As Joe Coleman puts it, *'the painting puts boundaries on something that is so overwhelming and disturbing [...] It is a way of controlling my fears and desires and housing them in that bordered object that has magical symbols on it, so they don't destroy me'* (Hensley, 1997).

The expressive art is a powerful tool to communicate the verbally inexpressible and, as we'll learn in the following case study, it can also help us become better communicators and find new creative ways to connect with young people through the safety of the metaphor.

REFERENCES

Anderson F (2001) 'Commentary', Rubin JA (ed), *Approaches to Art Therapy: Theory and Technique*, 2nd edn, Brunner-Routledge, Philadelphia, PA.

Argento A, Lieb R, Gates K, Kennison D, Haden-Guest A & Sargeant J (2003) *The Book of Joe*, La Luz de Jesus Press, Los Angeles.

Borowski J (2010) Joe Coleman Auto Portrait. Interview filmed at the Dickinson Gallery. New York City: October 28, 2010. Available on https://www.youtube.com/watch?v=jlvLIYpHF_o

Campbell TA, Pickett TC, & Yoash-Gantz RE (2010) 'Psychological rehabilitation for US veterans', Martz E (ed), *Trauma Rehabilitation After War and Conflict*, Springer, New York.

Colfer C (2012) *The Land of Stories: The Wishing Spell*, Atom, London.

Goleman D (1996) *Emotional Intelligence: Why It Can Matter More than IQ*, Bloomsbury, London.

Hari J (2009) The Child Who Kills is the Child Who Never Had a Chance. Article published in *The Independent.* Friday 10 April 2009.

Hensley C (1997) 'A look inside an infernal machine: an interview with Joe Coleman', *EsoTerra Magazine*, issue 7; 1997.

Khan M (2001) *Between Therapist and Client, The New Relationship* (revised edition), Holt Paperbacks, New York.

Kramer E (2001) 'Sublimation and art therapy', Rubin JA (ed), *Approaches to Art Therapy: Theory and Technique*, 2nd edn, Brunner-Routledge, Philadelphia, PA.

Kramer E & Ulman E (1992) Postscript to Halsey's 'Freud on the nature of art', *American Journal of Art Therapy*, 30(3), pp105–6.

Manley R (1998) *The End Is Near: Visions of Apocalypse Millennium and Utopia*, Dilettante Press, New York.

McNiff S (2001) 'The use of imagination and all of the arts', Rubin JA (ed), *Approaches to Art Therapy: Theory and Technique*, 2nd edn, Brunner-Routledge, Philadelphia, PA.

Meadow P (2003) *The New Psychoanalysis*, Rowan & Littlefield Publishers, Lanham, MD.

Milia D (2000) *Self-Mutilation and Art Therapy: Violent Creation*, Jessica Kingsley, London.

Moustakas CE (1977) *Creative Life*, Van Nostrand Reinhold, New York.

Pestalozzi J (1999) 'Containment and the body of the analyst: on psychotic transference in adolescence', Anastasopoulos D, Laylou-Lignos E, & Waddell M (eds), *Psychoanalytic Psychotherapy of the Severely Disturbed Adolescent*, Karnac Books, London.

Petros G (2003) 'Joe Coleman', *Juxtapoz Magazine*, California, Issue 47; November 2003.

Pfeffer S (1997) Interview with Joe Coleman, published in Internal Digging, the Catalogue from the Berlin KW Institut Exhibition; October 1997.

Pietras D (2013) *Murder of a Childhood: The Mary Bell Story*, Kindle Direct Publishing.

Robbins A (1980) *Expressive Therapy*, Plenum Publishers, New York.

Rogers N (2001) 'Person-centered expressive arts', Rubin JA (ed), *Approaches to Art Therapy: Theory and Technique*, 2nd edn, Brunner-Routledge, Philadelphia, PA.

Schauer M & S (2010) 'Trauma-Focussed public mental health interventions', Martz E (ed), *Trauma Rehabilitation after War and Conflict*, Springer, New York.

Sereny G (1972) *The Case of Mary Bell: A Portrait of a Child Who Murdered*, Pimlico, London.

Sereny G (1998) *Cries Unheard: The Story of Mary Bell*, Macmillan, London.

Shulins N (1997) 'Caveman in a spaceship', Article in *Spartanburg Herald Journal.* South Carolina; 13th July 1997.

Solomon A (2014) How The Worst Moments In Our Lives Make Us Who We Are. TedTalk; March 2014.

Taransaud D (2011) *You Think I'm Evil: Practical Strategies for Working with Aggressive and Rebellious Adolescents*, Worth Publishing, London.

Turner SW & McIvor R (1997) 'Torture', Black D (ed), *Psychological Trauma: A Developmental Approach*, Gaskell, London.

Van der Kolk BA (1996) *Traumatic Stress: The Effects of Overwhelming Experience on Mind, Body, and Society*, Guilford Press, New York.

Van Vliet J (2010) 'Shame and avoidance in trauma', Martz E (ed), *Trauma Rehabilitation After War and Conflict*, Springer, New York.

Webb NB (2006) 'Crisis intervention play therapy to help traumatized children', Carey L (ed), *Expressive and Creative Arts Methods for Trauma Survivors*, Jessica Kingsley, London.

Wieland S (1998) *Techniques and Issues in Abuse-Focused Therapy with Children and Adolescents: Addressing the Internal Trauma*, Sage Publications, Thousand Oaks, CA.

Wilson L (2001) 'Symbolism and art therapy', Rubin JA (ed), *Approaches to Art Therapy: Theory and Technique*, 2nd edn, Brunner-Routledge, Philadelphia, PA.

Wilson EG (2012) *Everyone Loves a Good Train Wreck: Why We Can't Look Away*, Sarah Crichton Books, New York.

Winnicott DW (2005) *Playing and Reality*, Routledge Classics, Oxon. First published in 1971.

LENNY, THE STONE CHILD

Sometimes our light goes out, but is blown again into instant flame by an encounter with another human being.

Albert Schweitzer

Hawaiian elders and keepers of the ancient wisdom teach that every child comes into the world with a beautiful bowl of light, a life-enhancing guide that nourishes his soul and accompanies him on his journey of self-discovery until it returns to its source at his life's end. However, the parable warns that as he passes through life the child might experience cruelty and sufferings. These hurts and harms are like heavy stones that fall into the bowl and block out some of the light. If his wounds remain untended, the child becomes increasingly fearful and the bowl fills up with more stones, until there is almost no light shining forth. And as the light slowly fades, so does the child. He falls into debilitating and rigid patterns of affect and behaviour, his heart hardens and he becomes like a stone, a living rigor mortis. For the light and the stones cannot occupy the same space (Wesselman, 2011; Riley & Malchiodi, 1999). Lenny was one of those kids, and his light had nearly gone out.

The stone child

Lenny was a 14-year-old adolescent with a stern face that was rarely lit by a smile. The week before his sixth birthday, his mother died from blunt force trauma injuries when domestic violence escalated. After years growing up amidst the terror of an emotionally broken mother and an abusive father, Lenny was placed in the custody of his maternal uncle, a materially generous but emotionally cold career-orientated widower who believed that a *'real man'* should *'suck it up'* and *'get on with life'*.

Lenny grew up to be a very healthy and physically muscular adolescent who spent most of his free time at sporting activities. His motto was, *'Just do*

it, but do it alone'. The pain of his loss, the lack of support and the terror he endured in his early childhood had cast a shadow over his life and blocked out some of his light.[33] Lenny had turned into a hard-hearted stone child. He was a sealed unit convinced that showing vulnerability or asking for support was tantamount to begging, admitting weakness and ultimately risking humiliation. He would rather remain emotionally starved than allow himself to connect with someone who might care. It was as if the only safety he could secure for himself was to discard his affective and relational needs, adopt an all-powerful and rigidly worn self-sufficient persona and single-handedly carry the dead weight of a painful past.

Every time new situations triggered past experiences, Lenny sought refuge in emotional detachment and thought suppression. There was a stiffness in his posture and a severity in his smile as if he was constantly holding back. Lenny's strong physique and rock-rigid demeanour often reminded me of the mythical Atlas, a powerful Titan sentenced to bear the weight of the world on his shoulders for eternity. I too also often felt weighed down and disheartened. Although he had openly shared he had *'bad memories'* and *'dark thoughts'*, Lenny had also clearly stated that he was a man and knew how to look after himself.

Lenny: *David, I like spending time with you, but I don't need saving, and I don't need your help.*

Yet despite his continual assertions that he didn't need *'saving'*, Lenny would never miss a session and he was always on time, but not on that day. It was a week before Mother's Day. Lenny walked in the room, acknowledged his lateness, said he had to take care of some *'personal business'* and calmly informed me he had just been suspended from school for threatening

---

[33] Although parental death is a profound loss, it does not necessarily lead to psychological damage. It is the lack of nurturing and support following the loss that can create deep emotional wounding, disrupt the child's sense of security and compromise his ability to shake off negative thoughts (Skinner, 2003).

behaviour towards his teachers and classmates. He then sat down, crossed his arms across his chest, tilted his head to one side and with smiling complacency asked,

Lenny: *So are you gonna try to save me again?*

I felt my cheeks burning with rage and frustration. After months of rejection, this felt like the proverbial straw. Lenny did not stop there, and he carried on telling me that I was wasting my time and that no matter what the world threw at him, he could sort things out by himself. His tone was less playful and more provokingly presumptuous than usual. I felt weighed down again. Hoping he might be able to explore his feelings and experiences as they arose in me, I voiced how utterly powerless I felt, asked if he had noticed how my shoulders slumped every time my offers of help were rejected and wondered if he could find meaning for himself in the kind of feelings I was experiencing with him. Lenny remained silent. For a second there was a sadness behind his eyes, but with a shrug and a disapproving grunt he pushed it all away.

I silently wondered if acknowledging my own powerlessness had reminded him of how he felt when he helplessly witnessed his father's rage towards his mother? Was he robust enough for such a direct exploration of his feelings? Did he even have the words? One thing was certain: we were stuck. As traditional talk therapy was clearly not working, I opted for a more creative approach. I decided to connect with him through the safety of metaphors, hoping it would facilitate our interactions and provide the necessary psychological distance he needed to confront and communicate anxiety-provoking material. I asked if he would be willing to try a little experiment and made it clear that although I could not guarantee the outcome, we might end up discovering something together. With a raised eyebrow and a blasé '*whatever*' he agreed. I invited him to pick up a large sports bag that was gathering dust in the corner of my office and asked him to carry it for as long as he could.

Me: *Let's pretend the bag is attached to your wrists and you can never put it down. You need to carry it wherever you go and whatever you do.*

The bag was opaque and Lenny had no idea it contained a dozen bricks I had permanently 'borrowed' from a nearby building site. He nodded and, to humour me, agreed to go along with what appeared to be a pointless task. I warned him that it was quite heavy, yet Lenny effortlessly picked up the bag of bricks and assured me that it was not *that* heavy!

Me: *I guess you must be used to carrying heavy things.*

Lenny shrugged.

Lenny: *And now what?*

Me: *Now we wait.*

Lenny: *We wait for what?*

Me: *We wait for something to happen.*

Lenny: *And what if nothing happens?*

Me: *Oh I think something will happen.*

Lenny, safe in his strength, stood still, carrying the bag. After a couple of minutes he tilted his head expectantly, waiting to hear if I finally had something interesting to say. I said nothing and together we waited in silence a little longer. A minute later, Lenny started to get impatient.

Lenny: *Nothing is happening! What do I do now?*

Me: *How are you doing?*

Lenny: *I'm okay.*

Me: *What about the bag you are carrying?*

Lenny: *Fine!*

Me: *Wow! You are definitely used to carrying a heavy load.*

Lenny remained still. We waited some more. Another minute passed.

Lenny: *How much longer?*

Me: *I am not sure. How are you doing?*

Lenny: *I told you …. Fine.*

Me: *My goodness, you're really used to carrying a very heavy load all by yourself!*

His eyes opened wide and I noticed the beginning of a smile!

Me: *What just happened?*

Lenny: *I get it! You're trying to tell me that this bag is like all the bad stuff I carry inside, like my bad thoughts, and that I need to empty it, right?*

Lenny was now wearing a huge smile on his face. He then tried to lift up the bag with one hand while trying to unzip it with the other. But the bag was too heavy, even for him.

Lenny: *Man! This is a big ass job!*

Me: *What do you mean?*

Lenny: *I have to carry the bag and empty it at the same time … it's too heavy … it's impossible!*

He started laughing.

Lenny: *Oh right, you are trying to tell me I need help!*

Lenny finally put the bag down, acknowledged that what he was keeping inside himself was preventing him from reaching his full potential and for the first time asked for support. Together we opened the bag. Lenny picked up the bricks, stacked them up and one by one labelled them with what he had been carrying all his life: his anger at those who earlier failed to keep him safe, his need to be self-sufficient, the guilt he felt for failing to protect his mother and his fears that he would turn out like his father.

Over the following few weeks Lenny and I further explored his needs to hold on to the hurts and pains of the past and what his life would be like without. And with time and support he started to let go of some and decided to hold on to others a little longer. But on that particular day, as the end of our session was approaching, we decided to put the bricks back into the bag until the following week. We sat down, had a drink of water and talked through the experience.

Lenny: *You know, I think that there are some adults who also carry a very heavy bag. And sometimes they try to empty their bags in mine. But it doesn't make their bags any lighter, it only makes mine heavier.*

He then paused, pointed his finger at me and with a little quizzical smile asked,

Lenny: *What about your bag, how heavy is it?*

Lenny was staring at me with such fixed intensity, I felt exposed. And although I was tempted to deny the existence of any woundedness and cover up my vulnerability with a false image of perfection, I thought that being honest about my experience would serve him best. As Brown (2010) comments, although vulnerability is often the core of shame and fear, for genuine connections to happen we have to allow ourselves to be vulnerably seen and known. Therefore a certain amount of self-disclosure from us, used judiciously, can foster self-disclosure from the adolescent and strengthen the bond of trust between us (Yalom, 2002).

Me: *My bag used to be very heavy, so heavy that I still remember the weight of it … but it's a bit lighter now … light enough so that I can help you with yours if you allow me.*

Lenny: *Who helped you?*

Again I hesitated. But after quickly assessing if revealing such personal information would be counterproductive or profit therapy and improve our relationship, I chose to answer honestly.

Me: *A therapist helped me to make it a bit lighter.*

Lenny: *You saw a therapist! But you're not mad!*

Me: *You're right, I am not mad, and neither are you.*

We were both smiling. We had reached the end of our session and as Lenny was about to leave the room, he turned around and said,

Lenny: *You know, sometimes I do it too. I try to empty my stuff in other people's bags.*

The Hawaiian tale of the Bowl of Light reveals that regardless of how painful and unpredictable our journey through life might be, the light never goes out. The parable explains that to reconnect with his inner truths, all the child needs to do is turn the bowl upside down. The stones will fall out, and the light will shine again brighter than before. For the light is always there and love is how we show it.

During this session Lenny reached out and asked for help. He began shifting his rigid point of view, accepted that it is union that gives strength and recognised that growth and success is a team effort. He started joining the dots between his past and present and reconnected with feelings and thoughts he had been defended against. And over time he gradually increased his capacity to respond more creatively and flexibly to new challenges.

But as Lenny astutely said, most of us also carry a heavy bag filled with the residua of past emotional pain, and sometimes we unconsciously try to empty some of its content into other people's bags. As discussed in part 1, a reinvestigation of our own childhood and adolescence considerably lessens the likelihood of us projecting onto others what we cannot admit in ourselves. For an empathic exploration of our unloved and unlived self is the first step towards the building of warm and nourishing relationships with those around us. And as for the question, when is a good time to look inside our bag and make it lighter? When the pain of holding onto old patterns and carrying dead weight becomes greater than the pain of letting them go, we are ready (Richo, 2008).

Conclusion

Primitive societies believed that the sacrificial immurement of a child during the completion of a construction project would win them the favour of the gods and protect the structure from evil spirits (Baring-Gould, 1892). Similarly, in order to survive emotional annihilation, children raised against a backdrop of fear and shame, wall in their needy, love-seeking self into the oubliettes of the psyche and surrender their autonomy to the will of the authority they are obligated to obey. Yet hope remains, although the shamed and wounded child of their early years can no longer voice his fears and his needs, the creative media, together with the facilitation of a safe environment, can bypass the protective psychological defences and give a voice to the quiet emotions. For not only is symbolic expression a rich window to the world of emotionally wounded individuals, but with adolescents it is often the only window available to us (Riley & Malchiodi, 1999).

Like Lenny, most adolescents whose sense of safety has been shattered are caught between two positions. On the one hand they long for warmth, but on the other they fear closeness. Like porcupines on a cold day wishing they could huddle but too afraid of pricking one another with their quills, they approach love with one foot on the accelerator and the other one on the brake. In chapters 20 and 21, we will explore how to reconcile their inner conflicts, but first, let us briefly revisit the approaches discussed so far in this book and examine how they can help us survive potentially explosive encounters with adolescents who use rage to manage their fears.

REFERENCES

Baring-Gould S (2010) *Strange Survivals: Some Chapters in the History of Man*, Kessinger Publishing, Montana (first published in 1892).

Brown B (2010) *The Gift of Imperfection*, Hazelden Information & Educational Services, Center City, MN.

Richo D (2008) *When the Past Is Present: Healing the Emotional Wounds that Sabotage Our Relationships*, Shambala, Boston, MA.

Riley S & Malchiodi C (1999) *Art Therapy with Adolescents*, Jessica Kingsley, London.

Skinner A, Fritz JJ, & Mwonya R (2003) 'Understanding the psychological and emotional needs of AIDS orphans in Africa', Singhal A & Howard S (eds), *The Children of Africa Confront Aids: From Vulnerability to Possibility*, Ohio University Press, Ohio.

Wesselman H (2011) *The Bowl of Light: Ancestral Wisdom from a Hawaiian Shaman*, Sounds True, Boulder, CO.

Yalom I (2002) *The Gift of Therapy: Reflections on Being a Therapist*, Piatkus Books, London.

THE RULES OF ENGAGEMENT

If there's a hell you might want to go there for a little rest and recreation.

Col. Quaritch, played by Stephan Lang
(James Cameron. *Avatar*, Twentieth Century Fox, 2009)

In the midst of the Vietnam War, Ho Van Than disappeared into the jungle with his two-year-old boy after their village was bombed by the US air force, killing his wife and two other sons. The pair stayed in deep social isolation for four decades. They survived by foraging for fruits and vegetables, lived in a 20-foot-high tree house and hid every time they saw someone approaching. According to the *Thanh Nien News*, a family member who knew of Ho Van Than and his son's whereabouts had tried to persuade them to return to civilisation after the war had ended, but the father–son duo refused to leave their home and way of life. In August 2013, soon after the local authorities brought them back to society, 82-year-old Than, in spite of his age and poor health, refused to eat or drink and made several attempts to escape and return to the jungle. Although Vietnam was at peace and unrecognisable from the war-torn country of 40 years ago, for Ho Van Than and his son, time had stood still. They still perceived their world from the standpoint of fear and needed to isolate themselves to feel safe. They feared in the present a threat that no longer existed.

Similarly, many adolescents who endured severe stress in their early years remain trapped in the nightmare of their past. Their views of the world as a cruel and persecutory place populated by heartless and dangerous people persist long after the danger has passed.

The battle brain

Children who suffer abuse or repeated lack of maternal care are raised to believe that the world only contains two polarised positions: strong and

Speechmark

ıl, or weak and vulnerable. They live in a world of kill or be killed.

:n is wired to perceive all relationships as potentially dangerous, and their survival depends on adaptation and on constant vigilance. In fact, recent research by Dr Eamon McCrory at the University College London shows that the neuronal pathways of these children resemble the pathways found in battle-scared soldiers suffering from post-traumatic stress disorder (PTSD) (Batmanghelidjh, 2013).

The fifth edition of the *Diagnostic and Statistical Manual of Mental Disorders* (2013) lists four clusters of PTSD symptoms: negative alterations in cognition and mood, avoidance, hypervigilance, intrusion and re-experiencing. These symptoms resemble the scars of infantile deprivation and help explain the way in which many adolescents manage fear.

Negative alterations in cognition and mood

(Which may include persistent negative beliefs about oneself, others and the world and feelings of detachment and alienation)

In the early years of development, the mother is the world to her child. When he feels safe and the care is reliable and consistent, he experiences himself as the centre of a loving world. On the contrary, when the giver of life happens to be the source of his distress, the child develops a view of the world as a place of threat, pain and suffering. Overwhelmed by a sense of hopelessness and with no external support to help him manage his fears, he retreats into a distrust of life and seeks internal solutions. He puts aside his relational needs and relinquishes all control to a mighty Omnipotent Self (a range of defensive behaviours and attitudes) to help him manoeuvre in a world that doesn't seem to offer him any sense of safety or security. Initially this alliance restores some sort of order. It helps the child to adjust and survive intense distress, but in exchange it takes away freedom, autonomy and cuts him off from others and his true self. What offers momentary respite comes at a great cost in the longer term. It casts an all-encompassing

shadow over the child's life that further obscures his view of the world, keeps the love-seeking part of the self trapped in a prison of fear, thwarts the establishment of a coherent sense of self and compromises his ability to form healthy relationships (Taransaud, 2011).

Avoidance

(Such as persistent effort to avoid trauma-related stimuli: thoughts, feelings, people or situation connected to the traumatic event, and a reluctance to seek out support and form close attachments)

A child who has been hurt or let down by people who were the closest to him learns that intimacy is a dangerous business. The negative internal scripts and trauma-related internalisations, such as *'love is a death trap'*, *'life is a battle of all against all'* and *'I am incapable of inspiring love or affection'*, prevent both expression and awareness of needs. Although his wounded core longs to be held and to connect with others, his early programing dictates that he must conceal his vulnerability beneath a smokescreen of aggression and silence the softer feelings within himself. In other words, his survival depends on his capacity to fool both others and himself into believing he is something he is not, for *'when a person cannot deceive himself, the chances are against his being able to deceive other people'* (Twain, 1924, p245). Or as Smith remarks, *'a liar who believes his own lies is far more convincing than one who doesn't'* (2007b, p126).

Thus not only does he go out of his way to provoke negative reactions in others that will validate and strengthen his omnipotent fantasies (as an 11-year-old adolescent who regularly got into fights said to a colleague, *'the harder they hit, the harder I get'*), he also wages war against anybody who reminds him of the unbearable memories of feeling small, scared and helpless. Anything that has the potential to bring back the ghost of his traumatic past, challenge the survival kit he has been relying upon for many years or shake the foundation of his belief system creates anxieties and therefore must be avoided. For him, lowering his defences, moving towards a position of trust and risking exposing his vulnerable core would be like going into a war zone without any protective weapons. He gave his love once and it nearly killed him; he is unlikely to give it again.

His need to avoid any reminders of the traumatic event also explains why he targets the vulnerable and the helpless, for they remind him of that which is small and soft in him. While the cry of the victim arouses empathy for the individual raised in a good-enough environment, displays of weakness arouse contempt and cruelty in the affection-starved teen because he is ashamed of the victim in himself. In the words of Karen Horney, *'he acts like the man who chases beggars from his door because they were breaking his heart'* (1945, p69).

Hypervigilance

(Such as feeling constantly on high alert and always on the lookout for danger even when there is no discernable threat)

In his book *The Birth of the Mind* (2004), Marcus states that a whole raft of recent studies show that *'the initial organisation of the brain does not rely that much on experience'* (p33), that is, that the slate is not blank. He compares the mind to a book in which *'nature provides the first draft, which experience then revises'* (p34). In other words, we come into the world with both a need to be loved and an inherent capacity to love others; we are pre-wired for loving attachment and companionship, but this does not mean that we are fixed and immutable. We are malleable and it is our experiences that shape us and reinforce our innate predisposition for empathic sociability and compassion. Or in the case of the emotionally wounded child, they rewrite the script and override his natural desire to bond with others with fear and distrust. The imprint of maltreatment leaves the child hypersensitive to stimuli reminiscent of the original trauma and keeps him in a state of constant preparedness. In short, the threat switch in

his brain is always on. It is as if he lives under an invisible but ever present 'Sword of Damocles' (Cicero, 45 BC). And as Cicero's cautionary tale warns, there can be no happiness for the person over whom fear always looms. For although hypervigilance is an adaptive behaviour that previously helped him anticipate and prepare for the next strike, it now keeps him cut off from emotional intimacy, hinders the chances of any reparative emotional contact and prevents him from moving forward.

Intrusion and re-experiencing

(Traumatic memories and past hurts are re-experienced in the present, leading to emotional flooding, feelings of helplessness and outbursts of anger)

In life-threatening situations and moments of overwhelming stress, the emotional part of the brain responsible for activating the body's survival response system takes over, and the cognitive rational thinking part shuts down. So the traumatic experience and its associated emotions get stored in the body, but they are not processed, or dealt with, on a higher cognitive level. As a result, long after the threat has passed, both the mind and body continue to respond as if the trauma is still happening in the present (Nickerson & Goldstein, 2015). In other words, the traumatic memory remains frozen in time until sensory reminders of that memory, such as smells, touch, sounds or emotions, transport the individual back to the moment when the trauma occurred. So working with adolescents who have experienced deprivation and abuse can feel like tiptoeing through a landmine field littered with unexploded devices that are just as potent as the day when they were laid. An accidental slip-up sets off the threat alert, and all the buried shame and hurt from the initial injury bursts forth in an explosive way. Anything vaguely reminiscent of the original trauma triggers painful unprocessed memories and immediately activates a defensive counter-attack. This aggressive behaviour is an out-of-date response to a threat that is no longer present. It is the means by which they manage terror and conceal the shamed aspect of the self. Ironically, their protective aggressive response is also a cry for help. It is how they seek the acceptance and security that their early environment failed to provide. It is a form of unconscious communication, an infantile yearning to be loved and to have their fearful affects contained by an empathic other.

Yet this distress call has the potential to short-circuit the rational part of our brain and trigger our own fight-or-flight response. We may roll up our sleeves and engage in power struggles or ignore them and run away because it feels safer than confronting them. Either way, when we act on impulses and let the primitive part of our brain take over, not only do we forfeit all possibility for empathic attunement, but we also run the risk of re-enacting the dynamics that were played out in their early environments. In this scenario, both the adolescents and ourselves get trapped in a cycle of unending blame, conflict and frustration.

Futile fighting

The adolescent, whose survival depends upon a long-term commitment to omnipotent fantasies, lives in the ever-present shadow of the original abuser. It is as if the painful relational experiences he had to accommodate in his early years are now replayed both internally and externally. His inner world is a house divided. It is a city at war where a battle rages between the love-starved aspect of the self who yearns for warmth and safety and the protective omnipotent part that seeks power and control. With no means to reconcile the two parts, the only way the adolescent can cope with these internal conflicts is by projecting them onto others, thus unconsciously re-enacting the violent dynamics he experienced throughout his childhood (Taransaud, 2011). Beside, fighting with oneself is a lonely enterprise and inevitably a losing battle. Fighting with the world is more fun.

The emotional onslaught has the potential to leave us feeling completely helpless and powerless. We might be tempted to respond by shutting down our empathy and putting on an emotional bulletproof vest or adopting the

Speechmark Ⓢ

role of a distant bystander and allowing adolescents to get away with murder. But ignoring them does not bring change; it merely confirms their long-feared belief that the world is indeed a godforsaken place and that there's nobody out there to help them explore the source of their hurt. Or, to preserve a sense of competency, we might feel the urge to give in to force, demand order and obedience (by which we really mean submission to our own wills and values) and fight fire with fire. But returning violence with violence multiplies violence and only succeeds in validating the adolescent's negative view that the world is a malicious place populated by oppressive people. Furthermore, although such approach might feel like the quickest way to set boundaries and assert our authority, when we respond with a counter-attack we chose the very type of struggle with which the adolescent nearly always has the upper hand. Young people who have repeatedly experienced situations that threatened their sense of safety are well trained and battle hardened. They have a fight-to-the-death mindset and would rather go on a kamikaze attack than surrender the strategies they have learned through years of self-preservation. They are seasoned soldiers with a reduced sensitivity to pain[34] and a heightened ability to read our emotional states and detect warning signs of impending attacks. For, as Smith points out, in order to keep their protective persona, *'the unconscious deceivers must also be unconscious perceivers'* (2007a, p5). The basic idea I am trying to put forward is that, when it comes to power struggles, the odds are definitely against us. And by placing confidence in violent means, like the Aesop's eagle[35] wounded by an arrow feathered with one of its own plumes, we give the adolescent the means for our own destruction.

---

[34] A reduced sensitivity to pain, or pain agnosia, is associated with elevated level of stress-related hormones, such as cortisol, which triggers the fight-or-flight survival response and dulls the sensation of pain.

[35] The Eagle and the Arrow (Aesop). An Eagle was soaring through the air when suddenly it heard the whizz of an arrow and felt itself mortally wounded. It slowly fluttered down to the earth with its lifeblood pouring out of it. Looking down upon the arrow with which it had been pierced, it found that the shaft of the arrow had been feathered with one of its own plumes. '*Alas!*' it cried, as it died.

The rules of engagement

In her book *How to Avoid Being Killed in a War Zone* (2011), Rosie Garthwaite, an Al Jazeera journalist and former British army officer, brings together the advice of seasoned war correspondents, NGO workers, military officers and hostage negotiators (and even a Somali pirate) for surviving in the world's most dangerous places. Many of Garthwaite's tips can be applied when working with adolescents who use aggression to manage terror. I have chosen here to focus on five of them.

- Be prepared and tap into local knowledge.
- Don't carry a weapon and conquer without fighting.
- Learn to manage your fears.
- Don't poke your nose where it is not wanted.
- Communication is key so learn to negotiate.

Be prepared and tap into local knowledge

Our first priority is to collect as much data as possible to help us keep an open mind from an informed position. A knowledge of their individual histories, coupled with an understanding of the adolescents' psyche and the impact of trauma on development, fosters a reflective approach rather than an impulsive and reactive one. An awareness of what lies beneath their aggressive behaviour can not only help us see the world from their perspective and decipher their non-verbal communication, but it will also minimise the chances of us stepping on an emotional landmine and triggering explosive remnants of their past. A lot of information will come from their files, family members, well-informed teachers as well as from those who had emotionally bruising contact with them, but we can also learn a lot directly from the adolescents. Our first encounter is an opportunity to gather more information and lay the foundation for the working alliance by conveying the message that our only agenda is not to change them or their behaviour but to get to know them better. The wonderful Dan Hughes came up with a humorous scenario to illustrate this point. He says we can well imagine the

argument that would ensue between a couple if one were to tell the other, *'Darling, I've been thinking a lot about us, and I think we would be much happier if you changed!'* It is a fact that we do not like it when others tell us we should change, and unless we have a compelling reason to do so, we won't. Yet this is the message many adults preach to young people: *'this school would be better if you changed'*, *'this family would be better if you changed'*, *'your life would be so much better if only you could change'*. We don't like it and neither do they! So the first message we need to convey is, *'tell me about you, I am interested in who you are'* or, as Hughes puts it, *'let me go with you into those hidden parts of you and together we will discover who you are'* (2012).

But, as previously discussed (see chapters 1–6), finding out about the adolescent's history is not quite enough. We also need to explore our own attachment history and familiarise ourselves with what we have learned to regard as shameful so that when adolescents stir up all that has been dumped in the basement of our psyche, we can roll with the punches. To quote the famous Chinese military strategist Sun Tzu, *'if you know the enemy and know yourself, you need not fear the result of a hundred battles. If you know yourself but not the enemy, for every victory gained you will also suffer a defeat. If you know neither the enemy nor yourself, you will succumb in every battle'* (1910, p11).

Do not carry a weapon and conquer without fighting

Dealing with aggression or intimidation without using force in return does not mean we surrender and give into passive acquiescence. It means we find a way to challenge the teen's perceptions by responding in a manner different from the one he is accustomed to.

On the morning of 3 April 2003, during the early weeks of the Iraq war, a small unit of young soldiers led by Lieutenant Colonel Chris Hughes found themselves surrounded by hundreds of fist-waving Iraqi men lobbing rocks at them while shouting in Arabic *'God is Great'*. The angry mob thought that the

Americans were about to storm a nearby Mosque; a massacre was a gunshot away. Hughes could have muscled his way in, but instead, he held his rifle over his head, yelled, '*Everybody smile*', and commanded his troops to '*Take a knee*'. They did. One after another, the soldiers got on one knee and pointed their weapons at the ground. This gesture of respect, and Hughes's ability to remain calm in the midst of an adrenaline rush, immediately defused the situation. The Iraqis' anger subsided, they moved aside and Hughes ordered his men to withdraw[36] (Baum, *The New Yorker*, 2005).

When dealing with aggression, lowering our defences is counter-intuitive, and showing vulnerability can feel like a foolish gamble – particularly if we have associated vulnerability with weakness. But it is a risk we have to take, for it is only then that the adolescent will discover that putting down his weapons will not render him helpless. Vulnerability and the maintenance of non-violent discipline despite threats and provocations defuses tension, facilitates change and can bring a peaceful end to the cycle of violence and counter-violence (Sharp, 1993). Since a non-retaliatory approach and aggression operate in fundamentally opposite directions, responding to attacks with robust vulnerability challenges the teen's negative world view and his need to rely on outmoded coping strategies. This helps him realise that disruptive feelings do not need to be acted out but can be survived with grace, robustness and dignity. It offers him a glimpse at a brand new world he had never imagined could exist.

Learn to manage your fears

Aung San Suu Kyi, the Burmese politician and 1991 Nobel Peace Prize Laureate, was leading a group of students in a peaceful protest on the streets of Rangoon. As they turned a corner, they came face to face with a line of soldiers with their guns pointing at them. Suu Kyi noticed that although the soldiers had cocked their weapons and were ready to fire, they looked as

---

[36] Lt. Col. Chris Hughes's actions were filmed and broadcasted by CBS News. They can be watched at http://www.cbsnews.com/news/a-calm-colonels-strategic-victory/

terrified as the students. So she turned around, asked the students to sit down and calmly continued onwards. She walked right up to the first gun, slowly put out her hand on the barrel and lowered it. No one got killed. Whether we are standing in front of a gun or facing an adolescent trembling with rage, this ability to manage fear is often the deciding factor in a conflict (Elworthy, 2014).

Garthwaite notes that when two people meet they bring their baggage with them, their fears and perceptions, and that can lead to dangerous misunderstanding. As discussed in chapter 5, most of our fears can be traced back to infantile anxieties; they belong to the estranged parts of our selves, the wounded child in all of us who still longs for recognition. They are signals by which we recognise what we have not yet integrated (Richo, 1997). Acknowledging them considerably lessens their control over us. But this is easier said than done; very few of us possess Suu Kyi's clarity and calm determination. If we have not healed the pain of long ago, a well-directed insult can hit us where it hurts the most, knock us off our feet and our adrenaline pumped body retaliates or runs for cover. But between stimulus and response there is a space, and in that space is our power to choose our response (Frankl, 1946). This is a space to scan both our words and body language for disguised forms of fighting back or running away. This a space to pause, engage our rational brain,[37] ask ourselves which part of us has been triggered and recognise it for what it is so that it does not mutate into a hostile counter-attack.

To put it another way, sometimes our greatest foes are not hiding beneath hooded tops and baseball caps; they are lurking deep within us. And often,

---

[37] In a 1999 interview in Rangoon, Suu Kyi explains, '*there is a vast difference in the attitude of a man with a gun in his hand and that of one without a gun in his hand. When [someone] doesn't have a gun in his hand, he or she tries harder to use his or her mind, sense of compassion and intelligence to work out a solution*'. Research confirms that the best way to deal with aggression is to engage our rational brain. Bernstein (2001) notes that when under attack, if we do not give in to our primitive impulses but instead stay grounded and engage the thinking and rational part of our brain, we have an advantage of about 50 IQ points on our opponent.

---

the best place to deal with an aggressive teenager is not in the classroom or in the dust of the playground but in our own mind (Bernstein, 2001).

Don't poke your nose where it is not wanted

Although a bomb suit increases the wearer's chances of survival, no amount of body armour can protect him against blast injuries sustained at close range. Thus the aim of any bomb disposal operator is to disarm the device as remotely as possible (Loveless, 2010). Similarly, when working with adolescents and potentially explosive situations, we need to work from a safe place. As discussed in chapters 17 and 18, metaphors, analogies and the expressive arts provide the necessary psychological distance from which we can help the adolescent confront anxiety-provoking material while preventing the full-blown reactivation of traumatic memories.

I remember Luke, a 10-year-old child brought up in an abusive home. Luke worked with Jill, a colleague of mine. The first time they met he removed the head of a plastic doll and filled its body with clay, dynamite-shaped sticks. He then put it back in the toy box, faced Jill and placed his index finger over his lips as if to say, '*Sh, don't ask questions*'. No words were exchanged, but the message was clear. It was his way of telling her, '*Keep your distance, don't come near my shame, or I will explode and the both of us will get hurt*'. It was also his way of telling Jill about his fear of losing control and that although he might not have the words to express his hurt he could show it to her.

Communication is key so learn to negotiate

The inner world of the troubled and troubling adolescent is under the siege of a highly vigilant Omnipotent Self ready to launch an attack on anybody who gets near its hidden and vulnerable counterpart. In other words, the powerful dynamics that take place within the inner world closely resemble that of a hostage situation in which the Omnipotent Self keeps the vulnerable Wounded Self captive and in a permanent state of fear and deprivation

(Taransaud, 2011). Freeing the love-seeking part and bringing about peaceful conclusion is a delicate process. If we adopt the role of authority figure, call in the SWAT team and rush in with all guns blazing, interventions are likely to turn into bloody rescue missions and inevitably do more damage than good. But if we learn to negotiate and aim to establish a climate of trust and understanding, we are more likely to get the job done and avoid collateral damage. In short, we need to model our approach to that of a negotiator and find a way to befriend the hostage-taker, or Omnipotent Self; as the saying goes: the easiest way to defeat an enemy is to make him an ally. Of course empathising with the omnipotent gatekeeper and freeing the locked up emotions is a challenging task. Like any negotiation, it will take time, effort, courage and considerable resilience. However, if we create a holding environment; acknowledge and validate the adolescent's initial resistance to our attempts at communication; welcome all his emotions with equal warmth; regulate our own impulses to ignore, attack or surrender to unacceptable demands; and instead remain fair and grounded when under pressure, we stand a good chance of fulfilling our mission and eventually of being allowed free – or at least 'supervised' – access to the Wounded Self (Taransaud, 2011).

Conclusion

Sometimes, to survive is to be invisible; an alternative to invisibility is to assume a disguise (Smith, 2007b). In both nature and human affairs, particularly warfare, deception plays a crucial role in the survival of species. Whether the situation involves concealment or deceptive imitation, the use of camouflage and mimicry are cunning strategies that allow for both attack and defence. Similarly, for the child raised against a backdrop of fear, neglect and abuse, the ability to hide in a plain site and develop new behavioural patterns to adapt to his harsh environment is a matter of life and death. Like an undercover agent whose survival depends upon assuming a new identity and learning new roles, the emotionally starved child must negate his true self and, to blend into his surroundings, adopt a more aggressive persona, an omnipotent self modelled after the original abuser. Howell describes the experience as having one's own *'sense of identity traumatically replaced by that of the aggressor'* (2005, p165). In short, in the world of the terrified child, imitation replaces action. He meets the threat by identifying with it; he mimics what he cannot defeat (Massey, 1976). It is as if, long after the threat has passed, the child remains bound to the original abuser who now rules from within. Therefore the teen who has internalised the abusive dynamics that were played out in his early environment is engaged in a private war between his inner selves, and although bringing about a change is as difficult as the challenge of overthrowing a repressive political dictatorship, hope remains (Mollon, 2001). In spite of appearances and irrespective of the maltreatment and violence the adolescent endured throughout his life, the love-seeking part of the self still endures, waiting to be freed and re-engage with life.

Before we go into how we can help liberate the captive emotions and turn a dictatorship into a democracy, let us turn our attention to a dramatisation of such inner conflict. In the following chapter we will go back to youth culture and further our understanding of the teen's conflicted inner world through the classic sci-fi thriller, *The Matrix* (Wachowski, 1999). For, as Hort remarks, *'no matter how intellectually agile or wise we may be, all of our elegant theories will have a dull, empty feel if we do not ground them in the stories that captivate our cultural minds'* (1996, p32).

REFERENCES

American Psychiatric Association (2013) *Diagnostic and Statistical Manual of Mental Disorders*, 5th edn, American Psychiatric Publishing, Virginia.

Batmanghelidjh C (2013) *Mind the Child*, Penguin Books, London.

Baum D (2005) 'Battle lessons: what the generals don't know', *The New Yorker*, New York; January 17, 2005.

Bernstein A (2001) *Emotional Vampires*, McGraw-Hill, New York.

Buck S (2009) *The Big Book of Aesop's Fables*, Comlan, Michigan.

Cameron J (2009) *Avatar*, Twentieth Century Fox, Los Angeles, CA.

Cicero M (2013) *Cicero's Tusculan Disputations*, Harper & Brothers, New York (written in 45 BC).

Elworthy S (2014) *Pioneering the Possible: Awakening Leadership for a World that Works*, North Atlantic Books, Berkeley, CA.

Frankl V (2004) *Man's Search for Meaning*, Rider, London (first published in 1946).

Garthwaite R (2011) *How to Avoid Being Killed in a War Zone*, Bloomsbury Publishing, London.

Horney K (1993) *Our Inner Conflicts: A Constructive Theory of Neurosis*, W. W. Norton, London (first published 1945).

Hort, BE (1996) *Unholy Hungers*, Shambala, Boston, MA.

Howell E (2005) *The Dissociative Mind*, Routledge, New York.

Hughes D (2012) *It Was That One Moment: Poetry and Reflections on a Life Making Relationships with Children and Young People*, Worth Publishing, London.

Loveless A (2010) *Bomb and Mine Disposal Officers*, Crabtree Publishing, Ontario.

Marcus G (2004) *The Birth of the Mind, How a Tiny Number of Genes Creates the Complexities of Human Thought*, Basic Books, New York.

Massey I (1976) *The Gaping Pig: Literature and Metamorphosis*, University of California Press, Berkeley, CA.

Mollon P (2001) *Releasing the Self: The Healing Legacy of Heinz Kohut*, Whurr Publishers, London.

Nickerson M & Goldstein J (2015) *The Wounds Within: A Veteran, a PTSD Therapist, and a Nation Unprepared*, Skyhorse, New York.

Richo D (1997) *When Love Meets Fear*, Paulist Press, Mahwah, NJ.

Sharp G (1993) *Dictatorship to Democracy: A Conceptual Framework for Liberation*, Serpent's Tail, London.

Smith DL (2007a) *Why We Lie*, St Martin's Griffin, New York.

Smith DL (2007b) *The Most Dangerous Animal: Human Nature and the Origins of War*, St. Martin Griffin, New York.

Suu Kyi AS (1999) Aung San Suu Kyi on Non-Violence. Interview in Rangoon. https://www.youtube.com/watch?v=j1ZILd1fnxU.

Taransaud D (2011) *You Think I'm Evil: Practical Strategies for Working with Aggressive and Challenging Adolescents*, Worth Publishing, London.

Thanh Nien News (2013) Man, son brought back from jungle after fleeing Vietnam War bombs. Ho Chi Minh City; 8th August 2013.

Twain M (1990) *The Autobiography of Mark Twain*, Harper Collins, New York (first published in 1924).

Tzu S (2010) *The Art of War*, Cosimo Books, New York (first published in English in 1910).

Wachowski A & Wachowski L (1999) *The Matrix Trilogy*, Warner Bros, Burbank, CA.

20

THE CHILDREN OF THE MATRIX

Two lines intersecting at a point after they have passed through infinity will suddenly come together again on the other side.

Heinrich Von Kleist

(*The Puppet Theatre*, 1810, p414)

The ice cream truck wasn't a giant music box, eating spinach did not make me as strong as Popeye, Buddy the family pet didn't really run away and telling the truth did get me in serious trouble. All parents, including those who set rules that reward honesty, depend on elegant lies and creative tales to avoid conflict, promote desirable social behaviour or smooth the process of shepherding their children towards compliance (Fisher, 1993). As we grow older, most of these fabrications get dispelled; we surrender to reality and learn the disappointing truth. Yet our early experiences shape the way we perceive the world and still impact the manner in which we relate to our environment and ourselves, as the tag line for the post-apocalyptic mind-warp movie *The Matrix* suggests: '*Reality is a thing of the past*' (Wachowski, 1999).

The Matrix

Based on Plato's Allegory of the Cave (387 BC), in which prisoners are tricked into believing that the imaginary is the only truth, the Matrix is a computer-generated dream world that camouflages a war-ravaged earth and keeps most of humanity enslaved in virtual fantasy. Unaware of the illusory nature of the reality in which they 'live', humans are in fact grown in womb-like pods and kept in a permanent embryonic sleep. Born into bondage yet blissfully oblivious of the truth, Thomas A. Anderson, also known as Neo, is an emotional and social urban hermit who leads a double life. By day he is an unassuming cubicle-bound software developer, and by night he is an outlaw computer hacker, plagued by a vague feeling that reality is not what it appears to be. Very little is known about his formative history, yet it is safe to assume that Neo's early years were not without pain. His self-contained solitary lifestyle, his criminal activities and failure to conform to social norms as well as his lack of interpersonal skills and heightened hypervigilant state all suggest an absence of secure attachment figures, a lack of self-care and an early emotional development distorted by deprivation or coercive control. And as the story later confirms, like the rest of humanity, Neo is an orphan, the product of a suppressive and emotionless authoritarian system, brought up in a world of lies and deprived of maternal care.

The desert of the real

In a world ravaged by war, the Matrix Power plant is now the Great Mother of humanity, the source and sustenance of all natural life. But it is a cold, corrupt and deceitful Mother, incapable of love. It offers a fantasy world which presents as a secure retreat from the post-apocalyptic reality but in return quashes freedom and keeps humans in contented servitude. This Orwellesque dystopia mirrors the psychological survival mechanisms of the adolescent. It attests to how the affection-starved child uses fantasy as a compensation for what he lacks in life and surrenders his autonomy to a powerful Omnipotent Self to protect the vulnerable or Wounded Self from further danger. Like the Matrix superstructure, this internal survival kit regulates the type of information that reaches awareness and shields him from archaic terrors. But in the process, it also nurtures falsehood, perverts the truth and forbids autonomy. It provides the illusion of being tied to reality but keeps him sleep-walking throughout his life (Taransaud, 2011). In short and to paraphrase the French philosopher and mathematician Descartes (1642), the adolescent is a prisoner who happens to enjoy an imaginary freedom in his dreams yet suspects that he is asleep. Afraid of being wakened, he conspires with his agreeable fantasy and remains trapped behind a wall of delusion for the sake of survival.

The Wachowski brothers also give us a glimpse of the inner prison where the frightened and love-seeking part of the self is held captive. One of the most terrifying scenes shows an emotionally and touch-deprived baby imprisoned in a womb-like gelatinous pod hidden deep within the Matrix. It is a cold, dark and solitary underground world protected by an impenetrable defence system and void of everything that gives meaning and worth to individual existence. But against all the odds, hope remains. In spite of its plight, the captive wounded self is still alive, awaiting to be brought back to life and longing for what it has been deprived of. And this hardly perceptible infantile yearning for a warm embrace creates a spark that arouses curiosity and prompts Neo to question his beliefs and search for the truth.

The yearning

Caught in a fantasy world, after another night spent searching for clues as to what the Matrix is, Neo is awoken by cryptic messages flashing across his computer monitor that lead him to Morpheus, an enigmatic fellow cybercriminal and the leader of underground freedom fighters who knows the answer to the big question on Neo's mind: what is real?

Named after the ancient Greek god, the revolutionary Morpheus, like his mythical namesake, is an elusive messenger who communicates through dreams and can fluidly move between the real and the unreal. He explains to Neo that he exists in a fictitious reality: '*the Matrix has been pulled over your eyes to blind you from the truth*'; he offers Neo the choice between two pills. The blue pill will return Neo to the 'safety' of the distorted dream world he believes to be real, and the story ends where it began; the red pill will take him from the familiar into the realm of the unknown and show him the truth. In a leap of faith, Neo opts for the red pill.

Morpheus's purpose is to kindle a light that illuminates the darkness within and set those in bondage free from the prison of the mind. In other words, he plays a role akin to that of a good-enough therapist. As Kalshed remarks, '*Therapy is not about relieving suffering; it's about repairing one's relationship to reality'* (1996, p100). And this raises a question: what does it take for us to help adolescents choose the red pill over the blue one? How can we safely peel away the protective layers they have wrapped around their hurt, encourage them to reconnect with the unlived part of their psyche and support them to experiment with new ways of being?

The Morpheus's way

The Wachowski brothers' sci-fi thriller magnifies our understanding of the adolescent whose omnipotent fantasies act as a substitute for an unsatisfactory reality. But in real life, unlocking the hurt buried deep within the psyche is not as immediate as swallowing a red pill. It is a slow and laborious process that requires a strong and genuine working alliance. According to Rogers, the process relies heavily on our abilities to communicate warmth, demonstrate a consistent and non-judgemental attitude and respect the adolescent's capacity for growth. So rather than brashly challenge his perceptions, pinpoint the blind spots in his awareness and warn against the danger of one-sidedness, we need to aim to understand what shaped his view of the world. We then need to nurture the sometimes raw and immature emotions that have not been validated during his early years, contain and normalise his anxieties and patiently foster what is unformed. And this can only be achieved if we step wholeheartedly into his perceptual world and not lose ourselves in it (see chapter 16).

Morpheus's awareness and ability to hack into the Matrix system make him a naturally gifted mentor who has an intimate understanding of the challenges involved in freeing oneself, and thus someone who can inspire others with confidence and renewed hope. His capacity to freely go in and out of the fantasy realm enables him to get a sense of Neo's reality while remaining in touch with his own individuality. Morpheus's empathic attunement is the healing agent that mediates one reality to another and gradually allows Neo to free himself from his distorted reveries. This suggests that in order to put ourselves in the internal world of perception of the adolescent without ever losing the *'as if'* quality (Rogers, 1957), we

ourselves need to be unplugged from whatever limits our own creative process, such as our imagined fears and unacknowledged needs for acceptance, control or praise. And for that, we need to reacquaint ourselves with the pieces of our own lost history and embrace all aspects of ourselves. For, as Rogers notes, entering the private perceptual world of the other *'can only be done by persons who are secure enough in themselves that they know they will not get lost in what may turn out to be the strange or bizarre world of the other, and that they can comfortably return to their own world when they wish'* (1980, p143).

After swallowing the red pill Neo is freed from the imprisoning womb of the emotionless Mother Matrix. He rises from his slumber and with the support of his mentor gradually achieves a deeper level of awareness and a better understanding of his reality, but the truth alone does not bring freedom. Similarly in our work with adolescents, although bringing a light into the darkness is an essential step of the process, an awareness of the conflicts raging within does not bring harmony; or in the words of Morpheus, *'sooner or later you're going to realize just as I did that there's a difference between knowing the path and walking the path'*.

The interplay of opposites

Empathic attunement provides a bridge between subjective realities and connects the seemingly unconnected. It allows us to forge an emotional resemblance with the adolescent and see the world from his perspective. It facilitates dialogue, conveys understanding, promotes trust and therefore fosters the building of a rapport with both the omnipotent self and with his wounded counterpart. It is through this process that the young person will gradually become aware and more accepting of the conflicting forces that exist within his inner world. However, a conceptual notion of the survival kit he has relied upon does not heal the chasm between the selves. For the conflict to be resolved, both parts need to be encouraged to interact with one another until they find a way to coexist and cooperate with each other to achieve a fuller, more creative response to life events.

Jung describes life as a dynamic interplay of conflicting yet complimentary forces and concludes that the psyche, like any other energetic system, is dependent on the tension of opposites (1959). We all possess a community of selves competing or acting together: we can be caring and cruel, creative and destructive, defended and vulnerable. Self-realisation and harmonious living implies not only an acceptance of the pluralities in our selves but also a confrontation between both positions and a reconciliation of differences.

Jung's belief is echoed by the Wachowksi brothers. Neo's polar opposite is personified by Agent Smith. Smith is a powerful computer program created to eliminate any threat that may disrupt the system of control generated by the Matrix superstructure. He is an emotionless artificial intelligence designed to keep the nightmare alive, to terrorise and destroy all hopes of ever re-engaging with life. His greatest power resides in his ability to absorb and assimilate the memories, experiences and characteristics of his victims.

Smith and Neo are an accurate representation of the adolescent's inner selves as well as their interactions: an orphaned self under the powerful spell of a powerful agent who forbids growth, creative freedom and autonomy. So while Neo symbolises the vulnerable love-seeking self awakened from his slumber after years of exile, Smith personifies resistance to change and creative living. He embodies the rigid and omnipotent persona the adolescent puts on to protect against further potential painful and traumatic experiences.

But in spite of appearances, these forces are complimentary. They are both the children of a cold and unresponsive Mother living in a fragmented and chaotic world. They represent one single body, one whole that has been split in two pieces yet strives to coalesce; they are conflicting elements that somehow seek to reunite.

This is amplified in the third instalment of the Wachowski's trilogy, when Neo is finally told about the true nature of Smith, '*He is you. Your opposite,*

your negative, the result of the equation trying to balance itself out'. In other words, as Jung states, *'the self is a complexion oppositorum precisely because there can be no reality without polarity'* (1959, p269), and for the conflict to end, the equation must be balanced, for life is born of the sparks of opposites. When thesis and antithesis collide, that is when the real adventure truly begins. After an interminable battle in mid-air in which Neo and Smith hit each other with equal force constantly repelling each other, both plunge to the ground and realise that there can be no winner. The only way to end the battle is to unite. Smith plunges his hand into a calm Neo and absorbs him. They merge. The equation is balanced and their reunification sends a massive shock wave through the Matrix which loses some of its deceptive powers. In the last frame, for the first time in the film, the sun rises, life returns to normality and humanity awakes to a new world, a world in which freedom is a reality.

Conclusion

In the Allegory of the Cave, Plato suggests that the truth beyond the shadows can only be attained through empirical experimentation. He implies that returning to creative living is not a matter for intellectual examination but an emotional realisation; as Zinker confirms, *'we cannot push through a piece of learning. We can't chew the material and transfuse it into the [adolescent's] arteries'* (1978, p66). To help him understand the roots of his conflict is not enough. To be transformed the adolescent needs to experiment with new ways of being. His awareness needs to be magnified and reinforced. It needs to be lived through and felt from within. So, the warring parts not only need to be acknowledged, validated and held but also need to be encouraged to interact with each other and speak their minds until they can eventually rediscover their original state of togetherness. In the following chapter we will explore how creative dialogues and symbolic communication creates an arena in which the secret kinship between what appears separate can be rediscovered and where the different aspects of the self can safely communicate, learn to coexist and work as a team.

REFERENCES

Descartes R (1998) *Meditations*, Penguin Classics, New York (first published in Latin in 1642).

Fisher S & Fisher R (1993) *The Psychology of Adaptation to Absurdity*, Psychology Press, Mahwah, NJ.

Jung CG (1979) *Aion: Research into the Phenomenology of the Self*, Vol. 9, part II, Princeton University Press, Princeton, NJ (first published in 1959).

Kalshed D (1996) *The Inner World of Trauma*, Routledge, London.

Plato (2010) *The Allegory of the Cave*, P & L Publications, Brea, CA.

Rogers C (1980) *A Way of Being*, Houghton Mifflin Company, New York.

Rogers C (1989) *The Necessary and Sufficient Conditions of Therapeutic Personality Change* (1957) – published in The Carl Rogers Reader, Houghton Mifflin, New York.

Taransaud D (2011) *You Think I'm Evil: Practical Strategies for Working with Aggressive and Challenging Adolescents*, Worth Publishing, London.

Von Kleist H (2004) *The Puppet Theatre*. Published in Heinrich Von Kleist Selected Writing. Hackett Publishing, Indianapolis, IN (first published in 1810).

Wachowski A & Wachowski L (1999–2003) *The Matrix Trilogy*, Warner Bros, Burbank, CA.

Zinker J (1978) *Creative Process in Gestalt Therapy*, Vintage Books, New York.

21

TO TURN A DICTATORSHIP INTO A DEMOCRACY

We look forward to the time when the power of love will replace the love of power. Then our world will know the blessings of peace.

William Ewart Gladstone (1809–1898)

The child who grows up in a world that denies him love and safety, and who longs to be cared for, relinquishes all control to an internal figure that offers protection but in return demands unquestioning allegiance and unreflecting obedience. The imbalance of power between the fearful affects and the defences used to manage them bears a close resemblance to the imbalance of power that exists in authoritarian political regimes. Like many dictatorships that were originally imposed in the name of liberation from oppression (Sharp, 1993), the defensive organisation the child depends upon was first put in place to help him survive a hostile environment but gradually turned into an insidious and tyrannical regime. The metaphor of an authoritarian state run by a ruthless despot is apt. Like an oppressive and absolute leader, the omnipotent self rules through fear, deceit and coercion. To maintain his status and assert his protective authority he must keep the vulnerable part of the self cut off from sources of support and emotional closeness, hopelessly dependent on him and in a passive submissive state. So he restricts freedom, eliminates creative thinking, promotes the superiority of hatred, monitors all communications and forcefully censures anything that contradicts his dogma. In Mollon's words, '*this is characteristic of false selves – once created they become tyrannical, suppressing the indigenous population of the mind*' (2001, p182).

Louw (2006) argues that violence and oppression, which exists wherever disparity is present, can be dissolved peacefully when all involved rediscover their common humanity through what Africans call the spirit of Ubuntu, which literally means '*We are one – I am because you are*'. When reflecting on the relatively non-violent transition of the South African society from a totalitarian state to democracy, he explains it was primarily '*the result of the emergence of an ethos of solidarity, a commitment to peaceful co-existence amongst ordinary South Africans in spite of their differences*' (2006, p170). Thus, when working with adolescents who have enclosed themselves in an illusion of superiority, the work is political. When the inner world is in a state of fear, repression and duality, our role is to facilitate negotiation and movement towards democracy (Mollon, 1999). In other words, to restore peace in the adolescent's inner world we need to act as intermediary between the conflicting parts of the self, create a space where they can talk through their respective experiences and mediate the shuttling to and fro of arguments.[38] It is only through mediated dialogues and reconciliation activities that both parts will rediscover their kinship and eventually learn to cooperate with each other in responding to life events in a creative and unified manner.

But before we discuss the role we need to play, allow me to illustrate how reconciliation of differences depends on both sides' ability to communicate and rediscover their untapped potentials through one of the Grimm brothers' lesser known fairy tale, The Bearskinner – as retold by Schlitz and Grafe (2007).

The Bearskinner

'*Man or Bear. When a person gives up hope, is he still human?*' This dramatic prefatory warning introduces the protagonist, a young soldier who upon his

---

[38] As discussed in chapter 19, the relational dynamics played out in the inner world of the adolescent resemble those of a tumultuous hostage situation with the Omnipotent Self in the role of the captor and the Wounded Self as the hostage (Taransaud, 2011). In real-life hostage crisis, in order to bring about a peaceful conclusion negotiators use a similar strategy as the one described above. They encourage activities that require both interaction and cooperation between hostages and hostage-takers, such as sending unprepared food rather than ready meals. This fosters bonding because all involved must work together, or at least communicate, to prepare the food. And the more the captors get to know their hostages, the more likely they are to release them unharmed (Greenstone, 2005).

Speechmark Ⓢ

return from war finds nothing left of his childhood home and the people he loved. Heartbroken and forced into the night with nothing but the clothes on his back, he enters a dark forest unaware that the Devil is walking by his side. The old trickster lures the soldier into a treacherous wager, offering protection and great sustenance if he agrees to abide by strict rules for seven years. In exchange for a bottomless supply of gold, the soldier must wear a bearskin, never wash, never cut his hair or file his nails, and never ask for support or tell anyone of the bargain. He must also forsake his birth name and call himself 'the Bearskinner'. Should he break any of these rules, he will forfeit his soul. Grief-stricken and penniless, the soldier accepts the deal. He surrenders his autonomy, forsakes his identity, mantles himself in the skin of a freshly killed bear and sets off to enjoy his fortune. But, as the seasons turn, the bearskin begins to rot; the soldier's hair grows long, his beard straggly and his nails crooked and claw-like. After two years he starts to look like a bear, *and 'by the third year, he no longer [looks] like a bear but like a monster'*. Cut off from any source of support he sinks into a misery so deep that he is on the verge of forsaking his soul when a chance encounter brings a glimmer of hope.

He stumbles across a frail homeless woman and her newborn child wailing from hunger. She reminds him of his former self. Filled with compassion, he reaches into his pocket and gives her a handful of gold coins for food and shelter. The destitute mother who sees the world from the viewpoint of the outcast notices the man in pain beneath the rotting bearskin and offers to pray for him. The seven-year pact with the devil forbids the soldier to ask for help but nothing prevents him from accepting support from others.

From that day forward, the Bearskinner uses his assets to help those who are in a similar situation like him prior to his deal with the devil and in return accepts their support. By doing good deeds he reconnects with his own vulnerability and vicariously satisfies the emotional hunger of his aching wounded self by using the positive attributes of his cloak. In the process, the soldier-turned-bear also learns that both elements of his fragmented human-animal self have a purpose and that their hidden potential is released when they cooperate with each other. The acts of charity he makes and the blessings he receives in return bring about healing and reconciliation in his inner world, enable him to outwit the devil and finally find love and fortune to last a lifetime.

The union of opposites

Redfearn (1992), echoing the work of Jung, argues that an individual cannot be helped to move beyond his habitual way of being until he is aware of his inner conflicts. The '*I can't help myself*' has to be replaced by '*Yes a part of me wants to act destructively, but it is only a part of me*'. Yet an appreciation of the contradictory and competing forces operating within the psyche is not quite enough. The warring opposites need to be brought together and encouraged to resolve their conflicts through dialogues until an egalitarian partnership is established. So once we have gained the trust of both sides our interventions should focus on fostering the growth of a relationship between them.

However we can expect that the competition between opposites will be fierce and passionate, Nietzsche likens these quarrelling to '*wrestlers of whom sometimes the one, sometimes the other is on top*' (1962, p54). Furthermore, their pairing is likely to create tremendous energy. Just as the colliding of hot and cold fronts forms tornadoes, or a couple reaching sexual climax in one another's embrace, the coming-together of the conflicting parts of the self generates a psychic explosion which is often difficult or impossible to contain (Redfearn, 1992). The Arts, as well as creative dialogues and imaginative play, not only provide the means to manage and harness the energy that springs from the tension of opposites, it also offers an arena where a common bond can be formed.

There are a multitude of creative tools and activities that can be used to override conflicting disparities and facilitate self-actualisation, many of which

I described in my book *You Think I'm Evil* (2011).[39] The following case study illustrates one of them, the reversal of perspective experiment.

The call of duty

The release of the latest 'Call of Duty: Modern Warfare' gameplay had just been announced and 13-year-old Lucas could not wait to get hold of it. For him, playing war video games was more than a pastime; it was how he dealt with his father's unresolved trauma.[40] Lucas was a victim of what scholars who studied the after-effects of the Holocaust called 'transgenerational trauma'.[41]

His father was a former soldier, and like many ex-servicemen who witnessed the atrocities of war, he never fully returned home. Although he rarely talked about it, the memories and hurt he still carried within him seeped out and were often acted out on his son through emotional detachment, behavioural outbursts and inconsistent discipline. As Fromm remarks, *'what human beings cannot contain of their experience – what has been traumatically overwhelming, unbearable, unthinkable – falls out of social discourse, but very often on to and into the next generation'* (2012, xvi). In short, Lucas had inherited the unresolved and unwanted experiences of his father. He was regularly excluded from school because of his abusive and unpredictable behaviour, appeared immune to behaviour management strategies and approached relationships with more dread than the condemned one on his way to the firing squad. Yet, in spite of his relational fears, we had managed

---

[39] These activities include various modes of kinesthetic, visual and auditory expression, such as the use of imagery, metaphors, masks, art materials, music, boxes, stories, films, movement and role-play.

[40] Daud (2008) observes that children of traumatised parents manage their parents' experiences by creating fantasies about what their mothers and fathers might have endured. They then act out these fantasised parental traumatic experiences both in their playing and relationships.

[41] Transgenerational trauma, also known as intergenerational trauma, is a process by which elements of one generation's traumatic experiences are passed on to subsequent generations through the behaviours and attitude of parents (Lieberman, 2015).

---

to develop a relationship based on mutual trust and openness within which he sometimes allowed himself to be vulnerably seen. But Lucas was still at war with the world. He had not yet reconciled the part of him that yearned for closeness and the part that called for domination.

We met twice a week, first thing in the morning. He often brought pastries that he insisted on sharing with me, and in return I made hot chocolate for us. Sharing his food with others was part of his culture, and although it was a little unorthodox as far as therapy went, it served to strengthen the bond between us. It was during one of our breakfast sessions that Lucas said he had woken up early that morning with a dream so vivid it seemed real.

He described he was trapped in a lift with his back turned against a large shadowy figure that made him feel uneasy. When the doors opened up, the lift filled with light and Lucas found himself transported to Chinatown. While walking through the crowded streets, he recognised the martial arts movie star Jackie Chan. They both leaped up in the sky and caught each other in a mid-air embrace. They then sat down together to enjoy a humongous meal. But as they were eating, Lucas noticed that the shadowy figure was still behind him, silently watching his every move.

Lucas: *So what does it mean?*

Me: *I have no idea.*

Jung claims that dreams, like the Arts, speak to us in images and symbols that arise '*from a part of the mind unknown to us, but none the less important, and is concerned with the desires for the approaching day*' (1912, p9). Thus they can bring insight and clarify our internal lives. But no one can interpret someone else's dream, for it only has meaning within the dreamer's symbolic realm. All we can do is to provide the individual with the tools to help him decipher its hidden meanings. However, it is generally accepted that the plot and the entire cast of characters in a dream represent

different aspects of the dreamer's personality as well as his internal conflicts (Fairbairn, 1952; Blechner, 2001). With that in mind, I asked Lucas if he would be willing to identify with Jackie Chan and retell me the dream from the movie star's perspective.[42] To help him become more aware of the parts of his self that identified with this character, I invited him to start by saying: 'Hello, my name is Jackie Chan and ...'

> Lucas: *Hello my name's Jackie Chan and I'm a martial art legend.*

> Me: *Wow Jackie! I'm a huge fan. You're amazing! Tell me, what's your story?*

For the role reversal activity to be successful, it has to be lively. We must be willing to join in and play a part. In other words, we cannot be mere observers; we need to engage in the process and give the characters that the adolescent plays our full and undivided attention.

Lucas, acting the role of Chan, described how energised he felt when he met Lucas; how they enthusiastically hugged each other and how full his stomach was after the meal they shared. However he did not mention the shadow's presence. After we de-roled and re-engaged in the here-and-now, Lucas asked,

> Lucas: *So what does it mean?*

> Me: *I still have no idea! Would you be willing to re-tell me that same story but this time from the shadow's point of view?*

---

[42] Like dreams, stories that appeal to adolescents often find echo in their inner worlds. So whether it be a tale from a book, a film, a video game or of their own lives, inviting young people to retell a story they relate to from each different character's perspective, encourages them to reconnect with parts they have been defended against. It expands their emotional repertoires and brings healing and reconciliation in their internal worlds. A full step-by-step guide to working therapeutically with stories is described in details in *You Think I'm Evil* (2011, chapters 8, 9).

He hesitated. But after I reminded him he was in charge of the process and could stop whenever he wished, he agreed. I invited him to start by saying, '*Hello, I am the shadow in the lift*'.

Lucas: *Hi, I'm the shadow in the lift.*

Me: *Hi Shadow. So what are you doing in that lift?*

Lucas: *I'm spying on Lucas.*

Me: *You're spying on Lucas! Who are you?*

Lucas: *I'm his father!*

Lucas's eyes opened wide.

Lucas: *Oh fuck! It's my dad.*

Me: *It's okay. Take a deep breath and start again. This time start by saying, 'hello, I'm Lucas's dad', I'm in a lift and I'm spying on my son.*

Lucas: *'I'm Lucas's dad' and I'm in the lift spying on my son.*

I shook his hand with a slow firm grip and wondered if he'd be willing to tell me his side of the story. Lucas, acting the role of his father, explained his son had to be supervised because he was a danger to himself. He described how he carefully followed him through the streets of Chinatown and voiced how furious he was when we saw his son and '*that Chinese guy*' eat and play together.

Me: *You sound seriously pissed off!*

Lucas: *Of course I am! It's my job to feed my son. It's my job to talk to him. It's not that Chinese guy's job!*

Me: *So why don't you do it?*

Lucas: *Because I can't fucking do it. I went to war, don't you know!*

Lucas, as his dad, angrily recounted his wartime experiences. He talked about the friends he lost to both enemy and friendly fire and explained that what he went through was what kept him from being a father to his son. His last words were, '*I cannot love my son. I don't know how to love anymore*'.

Lucas smiled a sad smile and lowered his gaze. I took his hand, sat a little closer to him and we stayed in silence together. For as long as he could remember, Lucas never got along with his father. He always understood why he behaved the way he did, but that morning, for the first time, he felt empathy for the one who could not love him. As the end of our session was approaching I suggested we took some time to debrief and talk through the experience. Suddenly Lucas sat up and pointed his finger at me.

Lucas: *Oh my God! David, you are Jackie Chan!*

He had associated the part of the dream in which Chan and him met, talked and ate together, with our weekly breakfast sessions. But he quickly changed his mind.

Lucas: *No, you're not Jackie Chan. I am Jackie Chan. 'Cause sometimes when I see little kids outside the head teacher's office, you know, when they're in trouble, I sit with them, and I talk to them like you talk you me. I help them.*

He then paused and added,

Lucas: *And I'm the shadow too. Sometimes it's hard for me to be good because of what happened to me. I'm like my dad. I try, but it's hard.*

Although he initially identified the shadowy figure as his father, Lucas recognised that because he grew up with little experiences of loving and being loved, he also sometimes acted out his hurt on others. Yet, he also knew that, despite all the hurt he had endured, there was a well of love and strength within him. This session was a turning point for Lucas. Not only did he develop an empathic understanding of his father's pain, but he also became more accepting of his own and, in the process, recovered a sense of hope and connection with himself and his environment.

Through further explorations of his inner conflicts via creative dialogues and imaginative play, Lucas deepened his understanding of how his inner selves related to one another. He learned that they could both be a source of knowledge and emotional growth, and over time he developed healthier ways of managing his pain. And as far as his father was concerned, he realised that they were both alike but different and that who he would become was completely up to him.

Conclusion

The Greek historian Herodotus (450 BC) writes it was the custom of the Persians to deliberate upon affairs of weight twice, once drunk so that their decisions would be passionate, and once sober in a more matter-of-fact way, thus getting the benefit of two different points of view on the situation.[43] I am not suggesting we bring wine into our classrooms; the point which I want to stress is that to consider a problem from different perspectives offers fresh insights, increases self-awareness and helps open the mind to new possibilities. Thus, the idea is to invite the young person to examine a situation from two, or more, opposite viewpoints, with the intent of creating a forum where all sides can communicate and start to work things out together. The aim is to encourage the adolescent to empathically reconnect

---

[43] The German philosopher Immanuel Kant (1798) notes that the ancient Teutons also followed such practice. They formed their councils to wage war at a drinking bout giving full play to their passionate minds and then reconsidered their decisions in the morning once sober.

Speechmark

with his internal cast of characters, reframe their attributes and find value in both sides so that he can risk moving beyond old ways to a more flexible and healthier way of relating to both Self and others. Naturally this is a gradual and strenuous process. Adolescents who have traumatically bonded with the abuser of the past will not easily let go of the strategies they have developed to survive. For them it's usually a case of better the *devil* you know. This fear of change is reminiscent of what both Frankl (1946) and Powell (1969) write about concentration camp prisoners the day they were freed: '*When they were eventually released, they walked out into the sunlight, blinked nervously and then silently walked back into the familiar darkness of the prisons, to which they had been accustomed for such a long time*' (1969, p29).

The work will be demanding and the journey fraught with unexpected detours and many setbacks. To free the captive emotions, resolve conflicts and restore peace in a war-torn inner landscape is like trying to walk up a down escalator. It is exhausting and does not follow a logical sequence. It takes time and requires determination, resilience and a certain amount of faith. And in spite of all our work and efforts, we may not always see the fruits of our labour to fruition. But, as Zinker (1978) points out, although we might occasionally feel beaten down by doubts we need to have faith in the process, and sometimes, we just have to feel satisfied with having planted a seed.

REFERENCES

Blechner M (2001) *The Dream Frontier*, The Analytic Press, Mahwah, NJ.

Daud A (2008) *Post Traumatic Stress Disorder and Resilience in Children of Traumatised Parents: A Transgenerational Perspective*, Karolinska Institutet, Stockholm.

Fairbairn W (1994) *Psychoanalytic Studies of the Personality*, Routledge, New York (first published in 1952).

Frankl V (2004) *Man's Search for Meaning*, Rider, London (first published in 1946).

Fromm G (2012) *Lost in Transmission: Studies of Trauma Across Generations*, Karnac Books, London.

Greenstone J (2005) *The Elements of Police Hostage and Crisis Negotiations: Critical Incidents and How to Respond to Them*, Haworth Press, New York.

Herodotus (2015) *The History of Herodotus*, Vol. 1, Forgotten Books, London (first published c.450 BC).

Jung CG (2002) *Psychology of the Unconscious*, Dover Publications, New York (first published in 1912).

Kant I (1996) *Anthropology From a Pragmatic Point of View*, Southern Illinois University Press, Carbondale, IL (first published in 1798).

Lieberman S (2015) *After Genocide: How Ordinary Jews Face the Holocaust*, Karnac, London.

Louw D (2006) 'The African concept of Ubuntu and restorative justice', Sullivan D & Tifft L (eds), *Handbook of Restorative Justice: A Global Perspective*, Routledge, Oxon.

Mollon P (1999) 'Multiple selves, multiple voices, multiple transferences', Walker M & Antony-Black J (eds), *Hidden Selves: An Exploration of Multiple Personality*, Open University Press, Buckingham.

Mollon P (2001) *Releasing the Self: The Healing Legacy of Heinz Kohut*, Whurr, London.

Nietzsche F (1998) *Philosophy in the Tragic Age of the Greek*, Regnery Publishing, Washington, DC (first published in 1962).

Powell J (1969) *Why Am I Afraid to Tell You Who I Am?*, Zondervan, London.

Redfearn J (1992) *The Exploding Self: The Creative and Destructive Nucleus of the Personality*, Chiron Publications, Wilmette, IL.

Schlitz L & Grafe M (2007) *The Bearskinner: A Tale of the Brothers Grimm*, Candlewick Press, Somerville, MA.

Sharp. G (1993) *Dictatorship to Democracy: A Conceptual Framework for Liberation*, Serpent's Tail, London.

Taransaud D (2011) *You Think I'm Evil: Practical Strategies for Working with Aggressive and Rebellious Adolescents*, Worth Publishing, London.

Zinker J (1978) *Creative Process in Gestalt Therapy*, Vintage Books, New York.

SUMMARY AND CONCLUSION

The walking wounded versus the return of the repressed

*Community requires the ability to expose our wounds
and weaknesses to our fellow creatures. It also requires
the ability to be affected by the wounds of others [...]
But even more important is the love that arises among
us when we share, both ways, our woundedness.*

M. Scott Peck

(*The Different Drum*, 1990, pp69, 70)

Imagine a world torn apart. A series of devastating catastrophes has resulted in Armageddon. The earth is now a post-apocalyptic junkyard and human civilisation is on the brink of extinction. Locked in your basement, you desperately cling to life while wailing swarms of flesh-eating zombies roam your neighbourhood. But your rations are running low and you need to venture out to gather food and water. As you cautiously open the front door and peek outside, you come face to face with Zoey, your neighbour's 11-year-old daughter. She has turned into one of the undead, and she looks hungry. Your adrenaline spikes and your fingers close around the gun clipped to your belt. Yet something makes you pause from taking any further action: Zoey is still wearing her '*Hello Kitty*' slippers. This makes you remember that the little creature staggering hungrily towards you was once a child; perhaps traces of her humanity remain. You suddenly find yourself torn between two conflicting sets of beliefs: the foundations of your moral system dictate that murder is wrong, yet the reality of the situation suggests otherwise. Eventually, your basic survival instinct kicks in; you convince yourself that little Zoey has lost all her humanity, label her a soulless beast, blow her brains out and go on to live another day guilt-free; after all it is not murder if the target is not human. But labelling is a dangerous game, for, to paraphrase Søren Kierkegaard (1843), when we label others we negate them, and to dehumanise the 'dehumaniser' achieves nothing but increases hatred and multiplies violence.

While the above scenario may read like an impossible fantasy, there are similarities between Zoey the zombie and our perceptions of the hooded teens who roam our streets. Many of us view them as zombie-types staggering around in a perpetual haze, with no understanding of moral behaviour and little concern for the well-being of the general public. They too are capable of evoking negative feelings in us, such as pity, helplessness, fear and contempt. Many of us dehumanise them and label them as thugs and street vermin, icons of evil intoxicated by gratuitous media violence or outcasts destined for the margins of society. Yet many of us also forget that they are children – children raised against a backdrop of fear, neglect and abuse; emotional orphans brought up in a world of lies and deprived of affirmation, empathic attunement and maternal care; children who in the absence of warmth and safety learned how to survive, but not how to love (Taransaud, 2011).

Let's return to our post-apocalyptic scenario; the dead have risen and your neighbour's daughter, Zoey, is coming right at you. Hesitation means death or a condition very close to it. Your sympathetic nervous system activates the fight-or-flight response. Adrenaline kicks in, your heart races, breathing speeds up, blood pressure spikes, muscles tense and time seems to slow down. Within a millisecond you assess the threat and have the choice of either destroying it or fleeing the scene. However, neither of the two survival mechanisms would have been available to Zoey before she was bitten by a powerful creature and infected by the zombie virus. Too little and too young to fight off or escape from her attackers, Zoey's most likely reaction would be to freeze in sheer, abject terror and passively surrender her humanity to the will of her abuser. Similarly, a child raised in a hostile and abusive environment absents himself psychologically from a menace he cannot physically defeat or escape. He allows a powerful substitute to dominate his psychic life, while his fragile wounded self regresses into

fearful submission. In short, the terrified child mimics what he cannot defeat. This soul-shredding union forbids freedom and demands complete sacrifice of individuality, but it restores some sort of order to the chaos; it redresses the child's feelings of inadequacy and allows him to fit in a world he perceives as dangerous and cruel. Therefore, in the struggle for survival, becoming one with the predatory other is a necessary evil, a desperate form of protective imitation where authenticity and creative freedom are crushed in favour of a degrading alliance (Taransaud, 2011). It keeps the child bound to that which wounded him, sleep-walking through a haze of life, in a tormented state of hopelessness, doomed to re-enact internally and externally the traumatic events that shattered his early life.

Rewiring the zombie brain

Neurobiological research shows that brain development is experience-dependent and highly sensitive to environmental change (Schore, 2011). While safe and genuine interactions with a caring other strengthen the child's inherent predispositions for creative living, negative early relational experiences have an anti-developmental impact on the brain. Yet, as the young people discussed throughout this book have proved, hope remains. Experiences of terror and cruelty can be contagious, but so can love. Given the brain's natural plasticity, positive experiences that contradict a traumatised child's negative expectations can undo the neurobiological effect of trauma and help put psychological development back on track (Teicher, 2000). Emotionally nourishing interactions ripple back in time; they alter the structure of the brain through the growth of new neural pathways, heal emotional wounds and reawaken attachment needs. The bond of Love is the healing agent that breaks the binds of time; it kindles a light in the darkness and warms a wounded heart back to life. Like the walking dead, the emotionally malnourished teen is a creature of hunger yearning for the nourishment in the form of love, warmth and safety that he never received. And as both the classic fairy tale 'Beauty and the Beast' (De Beaumont, 1756) and the zombie romcom 'Warm Bodies' (Levine, 2013) emphasise, the spell will be reversed once the tortured creature sees his forgotten humanity reflected in the loving gaze of a caring other. Thus we must put our faith in the inherent human qualities of the troubled teen and, like a good-enough mother, find a way to contain both his anxieties and omnipotent fantasies, validate his alienating feelings, find the fragile beauty within the savage beast and encourage the conflicting parts of his self to respond creatively and flexibly to life events.

The wounded helpers

'He who fights with monsters should look to it that he himself does not become a monster', warns Nietzsche (1972, p84). And as most horror flicks confirm, in a zombie-infested world, the slow-walking undead is often a secondary threat eclipsed by the inhumanity of the living. These narratives invite us to wonder if the monster is apart from or a part of the Self (Davis & Santos, 2010). If it were not for their rotting flesh, hollow eyes and lumbering gait, the undead would look almost like us. They are both human and grotesquely inhuman. They are the estranged familiar that arouses both revulsion and fascination. They evoke unsettling emotions which Freud refers to as the Uncanny, 'that species of the frightening that goes back to what was once well known and had long be familiar' but 'was estranged from [the psyche] only through being repressed' (1919, pp124, 148). In short, these fictional creatures that populate the dark corners of our cultural imagination embody the return of the repressed, something that was supposed to remain hidden but has crawled back to consciousness in monstrous forms. They are nothing but distorted mirrors that reveal the immature and un-integrated aspects of the psyche that return in fantastic guise and ultimately invite us to reaffirm our connections with ourselves and others. For, as Feshami remarks, 'when the faces in the mirror look so much like our own, but are so inescapably different, we are forced to turn our view back in on ourselves to examine who we are and where we as individuals and societies fall short' (2010, p94).

Similarly, the troubled teen who conjures opposing images of depravity and vulnerability personifies 'the strange masquerading as the familiar' (Walton, 2004, p127). We do not always see him for who he is; we sometimes see him for who we truly are and fear him for what he might reveal in us. The waywardness of the antisocial adolescent not only muffles an infantile yearning for the love he was denied, but it also triggers our stored emotional energy. It abruptly reawakens memories of loss and longing, the untamed monsters of our childhood, the immature terrors and concealed sorrows that rage within all of us. And perhaps it also triggers all that is forbidden to us, our repressed desires to rebel against societal norm and archaic parental control. It catapults us down memory lane, into a dimly lit cellar cluttered with the unwanted memories of long ago, and sometimes we unconsciously 'parent' from those places. For, as McCarthy notes, 'we have monsters lurking in our depths, usually ones we are unacquainted with, and thus our children become acquainted with them via our fear and anger' (2007, p138).

Such intimate confrontations with the estranged familiar are nothing short of terrifying; they challenge our standards of harmony and invite us to search for truer answers. They are what Jaspers (1963) and Alsford (2006) refer to as Boundary Experiences, 'times when the carefully cultivated and regulated pattern of our life is upset by an encounter with something so extreme and unavoidable that only a transformation of our existence or an act of self-negating denial is possible' (2006, p9). And while denial poisons the truth, and finds target in others who reflect our disowned parts, granting hospitality to the unlived parts of our psyche reinforces our natural inclination for emotional intimacy and creative living. In other words, these formidable encounters invite us to retrace our steps back to where things went wrong; they encourage us to reconnect with our discarded parts and give to ourselves the acceptance, the love and the warm embrace we did not receive enough of, but still long for. As Ilani Kogan adds, to be free from the burden of the past, not only do we need face ancient monsters, but we also must learn from history, and 'learning from history means coming acquainted with *elements of the present by understanding what entered the present from the past'* (2007, p215).

The return of the repressed

In the zombie culture, it is the bite from a zombie that causes this gruesome transition from human to monster. Let us consider a different kind of contagious bite, that of love. Like an airborne virus turning the living into zombies, catching the 'love bug' could be described as an infectious condition characterised by an impairment of normal cognitive, emotional and behavioural functioning. But in that case, the infected do not wish to be cured, for the recovery is often more painful than the disease. Let's explore this concept through two fictional characters, Emile and Maud, who are in the process of ending their relationship.

Emile and Maud decided that it was the best for the both of them. The separation was amicable, yet the pain was not divided equally. Everything around Emile seemed diminished by more than half. After a couple of days spent in his self-pity corner blasting angry break-up songs to overpower the critical voices in his head, Emile pulled himself back together. He rejoined the land of the living, hardened his heart and decided he was done missing Maud. But like those party trick candles that never go out, unwanted memories die hard. At first, it was the sight of couples holding hands, an old cinema ticket stub found in a coat pocket, the T-shirt Maud used to sleep in and the smell of her hair on the pillow. Then gradually everything around Emile became a reminder of Maud. Every love song resonated with stories of happier times, and every sunset featured an old cherished memory. A thousand times a day, uninvited memories flooded Emile's heart and mind and sent him back into a black hole of despair. He searched for new pursuits to dull the pain of his wounded heart, but to no avail. And so, vanquished, Emile reluctantly crawled back to his self-pity corner.

Avoidance and distraction only work for a short term; the harder we try to push unwanted thoughts and memories away, the more they are likely to

return. As a child describes, *'it's like a boomerang – the harder you try to get rid of it, the stronger it comes back'* (Smith *et al*, 2010, p52).

We have all experienced the profound pain of a failed relationship, or the loss of a loved one, and like Emile, we may have tried to wall in our wounded heart to defend against further hurt and humiliation. But what we disown gains autonomous life and ultimately it turns on us. As the old adage goes, a wounded creature is most dangerous when pushed into a corner. In short, and to paraphrase Masters, if our concealed sorrows seem monstrous, it may be because we have treated them as such, keeping them from loving human contact so long that they have taken up residence in less-than-human forms (2013). Thus, before we reach out to form an alliance with the emotionally wounded teen we must reach in to ourselves and reach deep. We need to empathetically reconnect with our own suffering before we can relate to theirs, for only then will we be able to put ourselves in their internal world of perception and convey to them that although pain is inevitable, it can be felt, survived and transformed.

Conclusion

Zombies have dethroned most of the iconic monsters of the past and have become one of the favourite villains in 21st century pop culture. These cannibalistic ghouls, who with a single infectious bite transform their victims into their own likeness, not only echo the process of identification with the aggressor, the *'if you can't beat them join them'* defence, but they also embody the return of the repressed, the shame-based memories that lie beneath the surface of the waking mind. For, as Powell notes, *'we do not bury our emotions dead, they remain alive in our subconscious minds'* (1969, p44); they live on within us and in times of stress they crawl back to conscious awareness and interfere with our abilities to form and sustain meaningful relationships. It is as if there were hidden little workshops deep in our psyche where we create monsters out of a ready supply of fear and painful memories. Acknowledging them will lessen their control over us and strengthen our capacity to live harmoniously and creatively with ourselves and others.

When asked about the zombie industry that has sprung up over the past decade, George Romero, the godfather of horror flicks, commented, '*I expect a zombie to show up on Sesame Street soon, teaching kids to count*' (Maniscalco, 2010). It may yet be a while before the undead join Elmo and Grover and teach our children their ABCs and 123s, but until then, these creatures, and the ones discussed throughout this book, can definitely educate us on what it means to be Human. Their *uncanniness* invites us to loosen the ties to our perceived realities and reconnect with the alienated parts of ourselves, so that we can develop the empathetic presence necessary to help the wounded teen return to creative living.

REFERENCES

Alsford M (2006) *Heroes and Villains*, Darton Longman & Todd Ltd, London.

Davis L & Santos C (2010) *The Monster Imagined*, Inter-Disciplinary Press, Oxford.

De Beaumont MP (2015) *Beauty and the Beast*, Harper Perenial Classics, New York (first published in 1756).

Feshami K (2010) 'Death is only the beginning', Davis L & Santos C (eds), *The Monster Imagined*, Inter-Disciplinary Press, Oxford.

Freud S (2003) *The Uncanny*, Penguin Classics, London (first published in 1919).

Jaspers K (1963) *General Psychopathology, Vol. 1*, Manchester University Press, Manchester.

Kierkegaard S (1992) *Either/Or: A Fragment of Life*, Pengin Classics, New York (first published in 1843).

Kogan I (2007) *The Struggle against Mourning*, Rowman & Littlefield Publishers, Lanham, MD.

Levine J (2013) *Warm Bodies*, Summit entertainment, Hollywood, CA.

Maniscalco J (2010) 'Zombie King takes Brooklyn!', published in *New York Post*.

Masters RA (2013) *Meeting the Dragon*, R A Masters Publishing, Oregon.

McCarthy D (2007) *If You Turned into a Monster*, Jessica Kingsley Publishers, London.

Nietzsche F (1972) *Beyond Good and Evil*, Penguin, London.

Powell J (1969) *Why Am I Afraid to Tell You Who I Am?*, Zondervan, London.

Scott Peck M (1990) *The Different Drum: The Creation of True Community; the First Step to World Peace*, Arrow Books, London.

Shore AN (2011) *The Science of the Art of Psychotherapy*, W. W. Norton & Co, New York.

Smith P, Perrin S, Yule W & Clark D (2010) *Post Traumatic Stress Disorder*, Routledge, East Sussex.

Taransaud D (2011) *You Think I'm Evil: Practical Strategies for Working with Aggressive and Challenging Adolescents*, Worth Publishing, London.

Teicher M (2000) *The Neurobiology of Child Abuse*, Vol. 2, No. 4, Dana Press, Boston, MA.

Walton PL (2004) *Our Cannibals, Ourselves*, University of Illinois Press, Champaign, IL.